Moving in Cities

Moving in Cities

Brian Richards

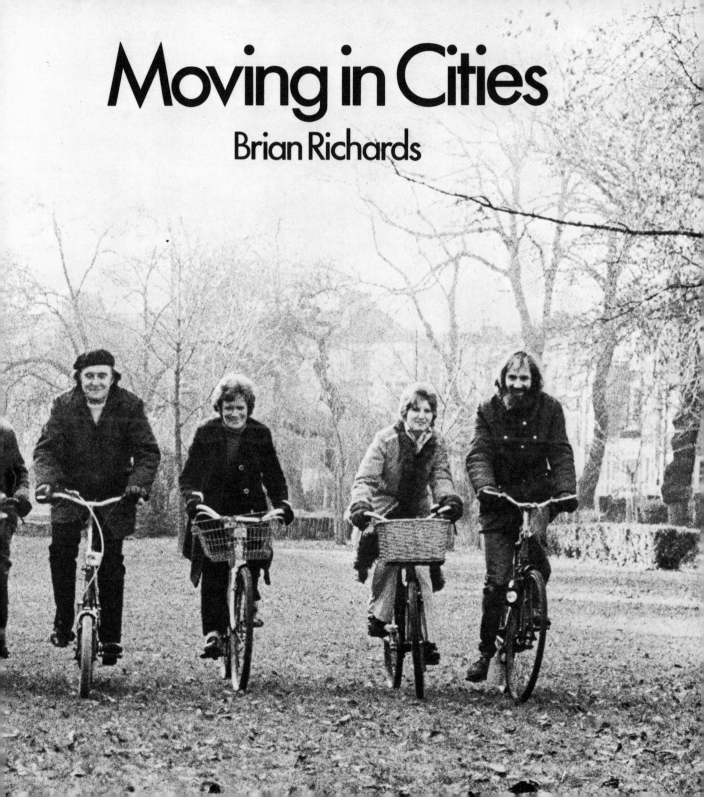

Edited by John Lewis
Copyright © 1976 by Brian Richards

Published in the United States of America by
    Westview Press, Inc.
    1898 Flatiron Court
    Boulder, Colorado 80301
    Frederick A. Praeger, Publisher and Editorial Director

Published in England by
    Studio Vista
    A division of Cassell & Collier
    Macmillan Publishers Ltd.

Library of Congress Cataloging in Publication Data
Richards, Brian
  Moving in cities.

  Bibliography: p. 104.
  1. Urban transportation. 2. Local transit. I. Title.
HE305.R53   1975   388.4   75-22380
ISBN 0-89158-513-3

Printed and bound in the United States of America
Cover photography by courtesy of
Archives of *Italy to be saved*, Milan

For Polly and Sam

Contents

7   Preface

9   *Existing Cities and the Future*
      Strategies for public transport

10   Movement in the City Centre

14   Pedestrian movement systems
      Walking
      Mechanical movement systems

21   Conventional systems

22   Advanced systems: Conveyors

29   Advanced systems: Vehicular

34   Interchanges

40   Goods movement: present and future

47   Residential areas

55   Leisure

58   *Transport Systems*
      Moving pavements

69   Continuous systems

71   Rail and guideway systems

84   Bus transport

92   Dial-a-ride

96   Car Hire

98   Cycling

101   Acknowledgements

102   *Comparison of systems*

104   Bibliography

It is eight years since *New Movement in Cities* was first published. While my first book* tried to show how new transport technology could help solve the problems of movement, principally over short distances, many of the systems discussed had either been tried fifty years or more before or were ideas on paper. This book still contains the more remarkable of these and also includes some of the considerable advances being made in the field today, while exploring what is being done to enable existing transport systems to work better, and how simple pleasures like walking in cities are being made more enjoyable.

The climate of opinion about traffic in cities, in some cases has turned full circle – almost too far, with often large scale road schemes being scrapped where some roads are certainly required. What must be found are good alternatives to providing for more traffic in cities and this book attempts to outline what these are and the ways in which public transport, both existing and new, can contribute to life in towns and cities accepting that the private car is likely to continue to be a system of transport which will remain popular and useful for many kinds of trip. Unless, of course, the present energy crisis and failure to find alternative fuels make the car an expensive luxury few can afford or even make it totally redundant.

What the outcome of these problems will be is both difficult to predict and beyond the scope of this book which tries instead to show the wide range of transport systems available today, and ways of using them which, were sufficient funds made available, could be both convenient and a 'delight' to use.

Opposite:
Forum Steglitz, Berlin a covered shopping centre on 4 levels where conveyors are used to change level and enter from the street entrance. (see page 22).
Middendorf.

* *New Movement in Cities* StudioVista/Rheinhold Paperback 1966

Nicollet Mall, Minneapolis completed in 1968 is a bus-only street used by over 550 buses a day, where pavements have been widened and the 12,000 vehicles which formerly used the street in one day removed.
Downtown Council of Minneapolis.

By far the most significant revolution in transport in the past twenty-five years has been the growth of car ownership and its effect on city form in North America has been encouraged by the almost unlimited funds made available for road construction. Mobility was made easy, for those with cars, to live and work in widely dispersed low density areas, and often resulted in the demise of public transport and the city centre diminishing in importance. The European city with its higher densities has not engaged in roadbuilding on anything like the same scale, and although car ownership has also resulted in dispersed travel patterns, the radial network of public transport, and its continued use, has maintained the importance of the central area.

Today there exists a growing interest in North America to redevelop the city core areas, largely as business centres, and with increasing congestion on the roads there is a revival of interest in public transport. Public pressure, too, has frequently caused a halt in urban freeway construction and San Francisco and Boston are among the many cities who have abandoned freeways in favour of improved public transport. This, however, has to be sold to the travelling public as a faster, cheaper way of travelling, than by car and is principally concerned with travel to the city centres. A number of Government sponsored measures are being taken to show how, for example, buses can operate effectively by being given priority on the often excellent freeway system, and these measures

although capable of being done quickly and at low cost still involve the politically difficult factor of restraint on cars. Many cities like Washington or Atlanta are already planning their transport around buses and new conventional rapid transit. Others like Denver intend to use new transport systems to supplement new and existing bus systems.

In the European city, while public transport varies in quality between countries, and in most is far from good enough to actually deter people from using their cars, the restraint imposed by the limited size of existing roads and the often high cost of parking plus lower car ownership has at least meant that people continue to use public transport. However, only recently have cities been active in improving public transport, and buses or trams, although they may now be given priority over other traffic on existing roads, with improved speeds can never match that possible on segregated rights of way. If the present resistance to new urban motorway construction continues it seems likely that many cities will ultimately be forced both to impose the measures of road pricing already considered in order to reduce traffic drastically, and also to engage in building or extending segregated systems of public transport, busways or track-based systems which will be environmentally less destructive than urban motorways and will provide people with better travel conditions than those they generally enjoy on public transport today.

Movement in the City Centre

Planning for movement and access in the city centre has in recent years often followed a simple planning concept. The core area is first defined, ring roads constructed around it serving car parks adjoining and several of the shopping streets made into pedestrian areas. This concept has been applied to many cities with core area of various sizes with varying degrees of success. In historic cities where the scale of existing roads is small, while civilised conditions for pedestrians have been made, on some streets, the extent of car parking and roads have often been so great as to isolate the centre from the rest of the city. Essen, Germany is an example of such a city which adopted this strategy. A centre containing a mile of excellent pedestrian streets surrounded by a six-lane ring-road and 8,000 car places, which it is intended to expand to 12,000. At the same time a new underground railway is being built and efforts are now being made to link the pedestrian streets, across the road system, with the neighbouring residential areas. In Munich, with a much larger

10

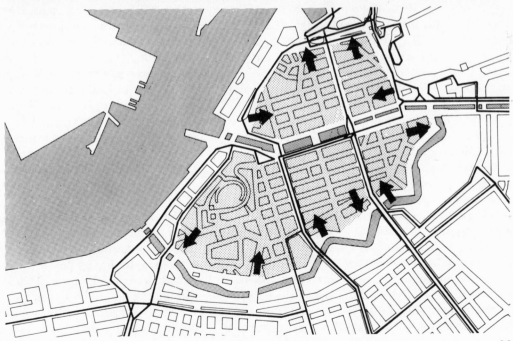

core area, well-designed pedestrian streets, over 800 metres long are similarly now being extended, by popular demand, but a six-lane inner ring-road, already partly built, has proved so destructive that it is unlikely to continue on the same scale. Unlike Essen, the number of parking spaces has been reduced from 16,000 to 4,000 spaces following completion of the underground. These two examples indicate the varying attitudes of city authorities to the question of accessibility, both by public and private transport.

One of the most significant schemes to improve the environment of a city centre in a short space of time and ease movement of public transport occurs in Gothenburg, Sweden. Here a scheme was implemented in 1970 after a preliminary experiment and much study, at a cost of £129,000, only four months after approval by the City Planning Board. The centre is divided into five sectors, each around 500 yards square, into which vehicular access is obtained from entry/exit points along the existing ring-road (see page 11). Buses and trams are allowed to cross between the zones (see page 72) and across the central area but no cars, trucks or taxis, although the scheme has since been modified to allow these to cross at one point. People can wheel cycles or mopeds between zones and a pedestrian network of existing streets is being extended across the centre linking each zone, and will eventually connect to the car parks off the ring-road, which are being kept to the present number of 5,000 spaces. The environmental improvement to the centre has been dramatic with some roads now carrying 70% less traffic, through traffic formerly amounting to 50% of all vehicles has been eliminated and pavements can now be

widened and landscaped. Road accidents have decreased by 20% with noise levels down by 9%. Reactions from the merchants in Gothenburg have been favourable with 66% of those surveyed in favour, although they would prefer to have more car parking, which, if large scale road construction to the centre is to be avoided and public transport run smoothly, cannot be increased.

Another city implementing low-key measures to improve the city centre environment and ease access by bus is Nottingham, England, which in 1972 abandoned its £100 million road programme in favour of a strategy which limits car penetration at peak hours. By means of 'traffic collars', situated on the radial roads, cars will either queue until road space is available for them to enter or be diverted into car parks, the driver then proceeding by bus. Buses will be allowed to pass through the 'collar' and proceed into the central area, moving on existing roads mixed with other vehicles, maintained at a volume restrained to the capacity of the road. Within the city core the measures of traffic restraint are enabling many streets to be paved over for pedestrian use, and movement within is being helped by free shoppers' buses circulating on a loop. Eventually existing car parks will be made for only short term use.

Many European cities of up to one million inhabitants are now adopting these severe methods of traffic restraint, aimed at giving over existing road space for use by public transport. While it is already accepted by most authorities that commuters should be encouraged to use public transport, service vehicles (see page 41) are a problem which remains, and how to deal with the

12

Kungsgatan, Gothenburg, part of the pedestrian network being extended across central Gothenburg. Following completion of the zone system, the environment for pedestrians was rated as the most significant improvement, in an opinion poll.

would-be car-borne shopper, more prepared to take public transport into the large metropolis than medium-sized or small city. One approach being tried considers that shoppers like commuters will be prepared to 'park and ride' provided that the service is good and the distances are short, meaning that parking at peripheral points around the centre, need not necessarily be within walking distance of shops or connect directly with the pedestrian areas. For example, in Atlanta, Georgia, the Town Flyer shuttle bus service operates as part of 'Project Intercept', running between two car parks associated with a stadium and a civic centre and carries shoppers into the centre. The estimated benefits from this kind of service, admittedly subsidised at the rate of $3,500 a month, is that 320 additional parking spaces could be eliminated in the central area, freeing the land for more valuable use.

Experiments such as these are still rare, as are the number of cities like Gothenburg practising measures of restraint in order to give public transport, buses and trams road space to move. European authorities, if no new road building is to occur, have no alternative but to restrain movement by private car which would be unthinkable politically in most North American cities. Here a massive injection of new road building in recent years and the extent of cheap parking on empty sites, has culminated in the very congestion, at peak hours, which the roads were designed to solve. Efforts are consequently being made to improve public transport, either by giving buses priority over other vehicles, or by the long-term measures of building new rapid-transit systems. New off-street parking such as that

proposed for Minneapolis in its excellent 'Metro 85' study is often planned to be eventually located adjoining, or built over the freeways and linked into the central business district by either elevated weather-protected walkways or mechanical systems. Los Angeles, for example is proposing to link peripheral garages for 4,000 cars adjoining the Hollywood Freeway with the Central City (part of the Bunker Hill Renewal area) by an automated vehicle system 1.7 miles long.

Theoretically then, such systems – shuttle bus, improved pedestrian walkways, or automatic vehicles, could all allow parking for short-term use (so maximising its use) serving shoppers or visitors, to be sited on land outside the central area, thus freeing acres of land now used for parking for other uses, and streets for the movement of buses, taxis and certain classes of delivery vehicles. In practice so much off-street privately owned parking already exists that short of imposing road pricing or a system of supplementary licensing (such as London's G.L.C. is now investigating), possibly no more than a 50% reduction in vehicles on the streets might be aimed at, still meaning that a considerable improvement in the walking environment would be possible, and leave room for essential vehicles to move.

13

Planning for the movement of pedestrians as part of the total transport system is now considered important by many city authorities in view of the emphasis being given to public transport. The two systems, the pedestrian movement system and the other work together, a traveller on public transport almost always walking further than one using his private car and given an improved environment in which to walk there is every possibility that the pedestrian can be encouraged to extend his actual walking distance, and the actual coverage of the city's transport system extends accordingly. Admittedly this is probably limited to day-time in the U.S. where only 10% of trips are on foot in cities compared to 50% in Britain and in particular to those cities with a favourable climate.

Walking

Today there is hardly a town or city in the Western World which is not actively pursuing plans either to close its principal shopping street to traffic or at least to improve it by widening and landscaping the pavements for people and so permitting only buses to use the road space. The existing traffic on the streets bordering the pedestrian area may be handled in several ways: it can either be squeezed onto the existing streets on either side as was done in Oxford Street, London, creating no major problems, or by building new ring-roads as has been described for Essen and Munich, which may prove to be environmentally disastrous. Pedestrian streets have proved popular with the public and with traders, whose business may increase by as much as 40% and the planners concern that a street may be 'empty' when traffic is removed has often proved unfounded. Munich's Neuhauser

– Kaufingerstrasse for example with an average width of 20 metres carried in June 1966, 72,000 people in twelve hours before pedestrianisation and 120,000 people in June 1972. People, like traffic, expand to fill the space available.

Ground level pedestrian streets have the important advantage of being quickly introduced at low cost and are capable of being extended as traders demand, particularly when new road building has not occurred. There remains the important factor of climate control particularly in those cities which have cold or wet winters and long hot summers. One possibility frequently done in Japan, as protection against rain, covers the street with a lightweight glass rooflight and Hiroshima, Japan, for example has an almost complete network of secondary covered pedestrian ways which cross the city centre. Usually these are built by the city authority who charges the shopkeeper a rent to pay off construction costs. Another solution which gives protection against rain provides light-weight canopies strung across the street at low level, and an example of these is found at Wuppertal, Germany, where good weather protection is obtained, with light and air at low cost. Finally there is the conventional method of providing canopies in front of shops, either individually or as separate structures. In terms of new development and weather protection there is naturally the excellent alternative of arcading, such as those existing in Bologna or Turin or constructing arcades, one of which in Gothenburg will extend to link with car parking at the periphery. Even existing arcades too are still proving popular and two splendid arcades in Leeds, England, have been refurbished and brought into the pedestrian

Elimination of traffic from shopping streets has resulted in pedestrians expanding to fill the space. Munich's pedestrian streets, shown here, are now used by nearly twice as many people a day as before.
Baureferat der Landeshauptstadt.

15

Opposite:
Aerial view of Karsplatz, Munich; new tram station in
foreground which links with underground shopping
below and the S-bahn stations at the lowest level.
Baureferat der Landeshauptstadt.

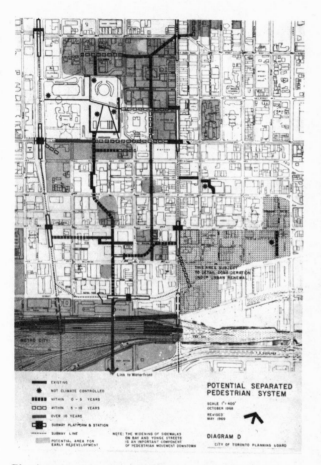

Phasing plan for a segregated pedestrian walkway system
proposed in 1969 for Toronto to run at ground and
basement levels connecting to metro stations.
City of Toronto Planning Board.

network. Planning strategies for pedestrian
movement may consider the use of different levels,
below-street level or elevated. Montreal's Place
Ville Marie development to-day represents one of
the most complete below-grade systems built,
evolving from the construction of a new
underground railway. Many stations in the
central area are linked to a continuous system of
underground shopping malls which are gradually
being extended across the central area, and in a
city which experiences extreme winter and summer
conditions the air conditioned climate of the malls
is infinitely preferable to walking at street level.
Toronto too is extending a similar walkway
system linked to pavement level, frequently
through plazas opening to the sky. There are
technical difficulties in providing for such
networks in a short space of time however and
redevelopment must usually take place before the
network can run through the block with the high
cost of crossing below the streets, usually requiring
the rerouting of services to avoid a change in the
walkway level. Alternative methods have been
achieved of providing for pedestrian routes, as at
Shinjuku, Toyko, where the shopping mall is below
the main road and connections are made into the
basements of department stores.

High level walkway systems at deck level exist in
the Barbican in the City of London and although
intended to extend throughout the city are at
present underutilised partly due to the poor
weather protection and the lack of escalator
connections to ground level. However, if and when
the heavy pedestrian movement flowing from the
main line stations can be channelled onto the
decks, it seems likely that they will be better used.

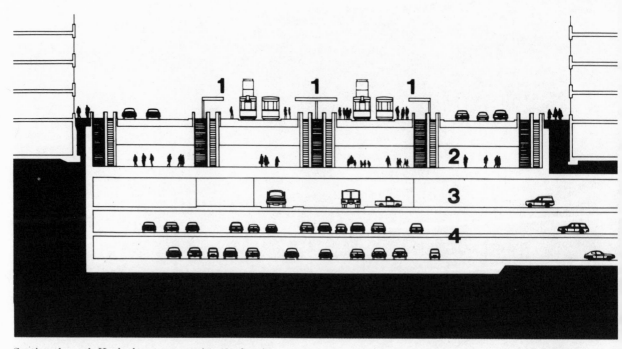

Section through Karlsplatz tram station (1) showing
escalators and stairs connecting the stops with the
shopping centre (2) below. Below this (3) is the service
and storage level and below this (4) 800 cars parked on
two levels.

1 TRAM STATION
2 SHOPPING LEVEL
3 SERVICING LEVEL
4 CAR PARKING LEVELS

ROADS
STAIRS AND ESCALATORS TO SHOPPING AND S BAHN
PEDESTRIAN CIRCULATION
TRAM LINES
1 CAR PARK ACCESS
2 SERVICING ACCESS
3 TRAM STATION
4 MAIN PEDESTRIAN THOROUGHFARE

Ground level plan of Karlsplatz tram station showing
escalator and stair access down to shops below.

Basement plan of shopping area, all air-conditioned,
part of which is owned by a large adjoining store.

18

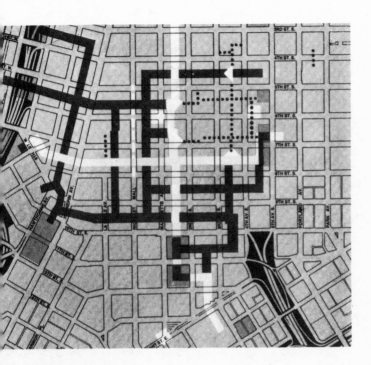

Pedestrian Circulation Plan
- Primary Skyways
- Feeder Skyways
- Underground Concourses
- Interchanges Between Systems
- Rapid Transit Stations
- Fringe Parking Ramps
- Enclosed Mall

Minneapolis Metro Center '85 Plan is one of the few which shows concern for climate, severe here, and the plan shows proposals for weather control in its central area.
Minneapolis Planning and Development

Arcaded shopping streets in Tokyo, where an existing street is covered with a free-standing lightweight structure, built usually by the local authority; shopkeepers pay a rent to meet capital costs.
Yoshio Tsukio.

Two important examples of elevated walkways exist at St Paul and Minneapolis where already seven air conditioned glazed bridges connect with lift lobbies within the city blocks and offer comfortable walking conditions in a severe climate over a limited distance and plans for extending these are being made.

The pedestrian systems described which provide for movement above or below ground are all both costly and long-term measures, usually occurring as part of redevelopment, and while it is likely that in existing cities the ground level will be that at which most pedestrian movement will occur, the possibilities exist for great variety and delight

19

Lightweight experimental roof covering a shopping street in Wuppertal using cables and plastic covering.

Arcade off Hamngatan, Gothenburg, part of pedestrian network being extended out to parking at the periphery in new development which will be weather protected

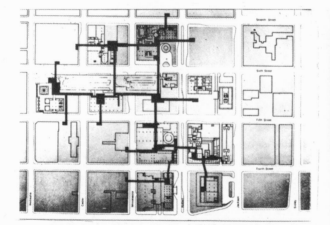

Skyway system in St Paul, Minnesota, showing how elevated pedestrian bridges are being extended to link the centre of a number of city blocks, resulting in shops being relocated at the upper levels.

View of air-conditioned bridge linking buildings.
Housing & Redevelopment Authority, St. Paul.

in the pedestrian environment by encouraging pedestrian movement at a number of different levels. This may grow naturally following the introduction of a new transport system, running either above or below ground. Also a wide range of opportunities exist in providing for a weather-controlled traffic-free environment for pedestrians and although probably encouraging people to walk further, it is still necessary to provide for other systems of movement for use over distances too far to walk.

Toronto is developing an underground walkway system linked to the metro stations and open plazas such as these connect the system with the ground level pavements.

Mechanical movement systems: Conventional

Internal systems of movement in addition to the longer distance systems may also be necessary within a centre. For example to connect to terminal facilities at the periphery such as short-wait car parks, bus or railway stations. Within a central business district shoppers buses may be used which circulate on a fixed route, usually near the principle shopping street at high frequency. Nottingham for example runs a free shoppers' bus at five minute intervals around the city centre which within three months from starting ran at 60% capacity.

Conventional systems, bus, tram and train can give good service for pedestrians, provided stops are frequent (at 400 yard interval or less) and properly sited, relating to pedestrian streets. Buses at present are still frequently both noisy, dangerous and polluting and their large scale also conflicts with the scale of a pedestrian street. Smaller buses are now being tried in some countries which are quiet, non-polluting and being low-slung are easy to board, have proved popular with shoppers and although taking up less road space than a conventional bus have the principal disadvantage of being of low capacity and unable to handle peak hour loading. Alternatively small electric road trains are frequently used within shopping malls and although popular, are unsuitable where pedestrian flows are dense.

Taxis are an important means of movement for people prepared to pay the high cost of fares and requiring to make random trips within a city, often carrying luggage or purchases. The vehicle could however be smaller, two or three seater and be non-polluting, and in addition larger vehicles seating six or more such as a limousine or minibus could, if encouraged by city authorities, play an important contribution to the overall transport system in a city. At present such vehicles are widely used in Mexico City, Moscow and Teheran where they ply on fixed or varied routes collecting or dropping off people as required, at a higher fare than a normal bus. Such taxis could be allowed to operate in a variety of ways depending on the demand, on fixed routes from points of principal pedestrian generation at peak hours or if equipped with radio as dial-a-ride systems on flexible routes at off-peak hours. Taxi stands located at frequent points within the city could do much to avoid the present congestion caused by cruising taxis and with telephones at each stand, combined with radios in the vehicles, could improve the efficiency of the total system.

Advanced systems: Conveyors

New systems of movement are now being considered in certain situations within cities, particularly where large concentrations of people have to be moved, where segregation from pedestrians is necessary and no waiting is desirable. Pedestrian conveyors are increasingly being used as an aid to pedestrian movement. For example, in connection with underground railways, the Paris Metro has two installations to help passengers interchanging at Chatelet and Montparnasse stations 132 metres long and 182 metres long respectively, running in subway. An installation at Tacoma, Washington, in a hilly situation, uses eight conveyors at a 13° slope within an arcade and in Sydney, Australia two 200 metre conveyors connect an underground car park to a shopping street. Conveyors are widely used in shopping centres to handle changes of level, where shoppers are using trolleys, and an excellent example of this exists at the Forum Steglitz in Berlin, a multi-level arcade of different shops, where a conveyor runs from the main entrance at street level horizontally, bringing people from the pavement into the centre of the building, thence shoppers can rise by other conveyors and escalators through all three levels of shops.

The 1959 Soho project by Dean and Richards (see page 26) was a study of a building type designed to be in scale with an urban motorway and to act as a generator for new development. The route building proposed had within it a series of elevated pedestrian malls which ran the length of each block and were interlinked by pedestrian conveyors running through them. This movement system linked to express bus stations on the motorways was intended to be built in stages and provide an extended web of transport and elevated pedestrian ways over the whole area. Along the shopping malls, restaurants, shops and cinemas would be

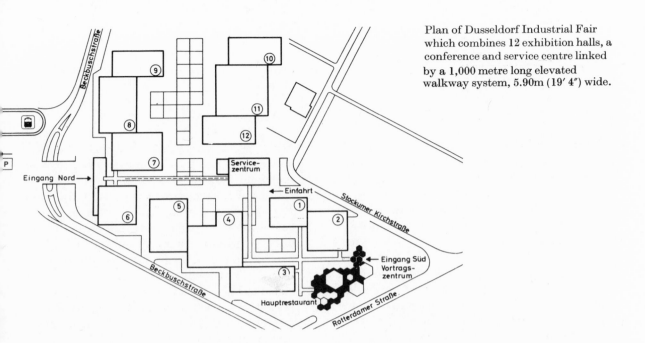

Plan of Dusseldorf Industrial Fair which combines 12 exhibition halls, a conference and service centre linked by a 1,000 metre long elevated walkway system, 5.90m (19' 4") wide.

The steel supporting structure spans 15 metres and erection was completed in 5 months.
Rheinstahl-Eggers-Kehrahn.

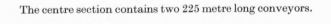

The centre section contains two 225 metre long conveyors.

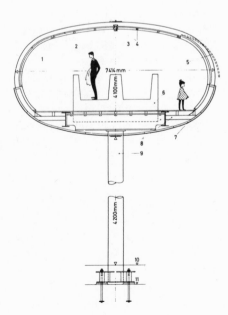

placed and multi-storeyed flats, offices or hotels would be built in stages alongside connected to the pedestrian network. Detailed design and traffic studies were completed in 1971, sponsored by the US Government, for an area of downtown Boston adjoining South Park station which comprised redevelopment of one side of a main street about half-a-mile in length. This consisted of a continuous elevated pedestrian walkway system running in an arcade supplemented by a series of pedestrian conveyors. Studies were also done as part of the Center City Transportation Project for Seattle which showed how a conveyor system running elevated in a series of separate lengths could be installed to run elevated across the central area connecting two generators of pedestrian traffic at either end, the Ferry Terminal at one and a car park at the other and act as a distributor to the offices and shops along its route. Both in the Seattle Study and that for Boston, it was suggested that higher speed conveyors could be considered when they were available in the future.

Conveyors moving at $1\frac{1}{2}$ mph are suitable for horizontal travel distances up to 200′ as they do have the advantage of speed, provided they can be walked on, psychologically reducing travel distances. However, new developments in high speed conveyors such as the Speedaway system make safe movement at up to 10 mph possible, and lengths of 1,000 metres or more can be provided. Because of the need to cross the system, such conveyors will run either elevated above the street or below ground in subway and will normally be placed end to end to allow boarding every 400 metres. The Speedaway was studied in 1971 to run above the new London Bridge, designed to take such a structure at a future date. The proposal used twin high-speed conveyors 400 metres long, operating within an air-conditioned enclosure and connected at either end with elevated pedestrian decks. This route, represents one of the densest corridors of movement in London, 11,000 people at peak hour, morning and evening from a main line station to the office district, and pedestrians who now walk at bridge level have to cross the dense traffic at the north end. Future extensions were planned, to link with a main line station to the north and it was estimated that as the route extended, two sections of the Underground might be relieved of peak loading and in addition a shuttle bus system could be eliminated.

View of system running over main road consists of 10-person cars running automatically at 15 mph within glass enclosed tube, slowing at stations at 400 yard intervals.

roject for Oxford Street, London
966–68. Elevated secondary
ovement system constructed in
rst stage over main traffic roads
ith station connecting directly
o underground.

Left:
Acquisition of property behind main road permits eventual construction of route building which has shopping mall combined with secondary movement system for pedestrians.

View of pedestrian mall showing people leaving continuously moving system by conveyor.

Soho Project by Dean and Richards 1959. Showing urban
motorways having express bus stations linked by route
building with built-in secondary transport system
within and continuous shopping malls.

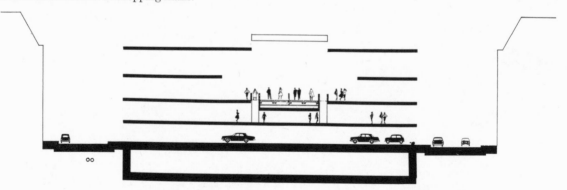

Section through Soho project route building showing
shopping mall and secondary transport system.

RAPID TRANSIT
CONCOURSE
PASSENGER CONVEYORS
HOUSING

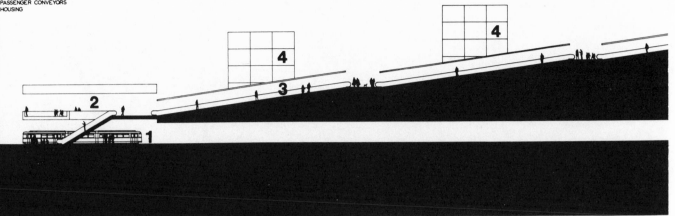

Conveyors are used to link the pedestrian approach to high rise housing (4) situated on a hillside to the tramway station (2) of Galileis Gata, in a Gothenburg suburb. Gothenburg's transport department does not accept a walking distance of more than 400 metres from a transit stop to multi-storeyed housing, and if a change of level is involved work on a formula that for every metre of rise, 10 metres is added to the walking distance and so were able to justify installation of conveyors connecting to the tram station.

View of conveyors running from tram station.

Internal view along conveyors.
Goteborgs Sparvagar.

Plan showing capability of Speedaway links
crossing the Thames, connecting existing
underground stations on the north bank with
land on the south now being developed.
Consultant: Brian Richards.

Interior view along system, which can carry
up to 10,000 people an hour in each
direction, or be operated with both
conveyors running the same way to handle
peak hour movement.
Dunlop Transportation Systems Division.

Perspective showing study for 2-way Speedaway system in an air conditioned tube running above the new London Bridge, already designed to take the loading and supports.

Advanced systems: Vehicular

A wide range of automatically controlled vehicle systems is now available for use within central areas which may either be used for pedestrian movement within the area to connect with peripheral car parks or with residential areas. The systems themselves are of basically two types, continuous operation, using cabins requiring no waiting at boarding points, such as the Carveyor, (see page 69) or intermittent systems using cabins running as trains or individually which stop at platforms at frequent intervals automatically or as required by the traveller (see PRT systems page 79). All these systems require to run on a track segregated from pedestrians and vehicles and are usually located above or below ground. Running in a subway construction costs may be three times higher than an elevated system and in either location an important factor for the pedestrian is the close spacing of boarding points (around 400 yard intervals) and the ease with which they can be reached by escalator or lift, from ground level. Studies undertaken in 1973 for Mid-Manhattan, New York, by Kaiser Engineers indicated the potential of a wide range of different systems, in the context of an extended central area already well served by five underground railways running the length of Manhattan but badly served by transport for crosstown movement, particularly on the west side. Improved access to the west side was intended to be provided by a system running crosstown underground – linked to the subway stations, and encouraging new development such as a conference centre to be built on the west side. One segregated vehicle system was shown to run the two mile distance crosstown at 13.7 mph (average speed) while a surface level bus running on one-way bus only streets could only average 7.2 mph. The bus system would however only cost one-fifth of the vehicular system to install, although to carry an equivalent capacity would have required to be run at 30 second intervals, barely sufficient for pedestrians to cross the road.

Several vehicular systems are already in use as shuttle systems such as that operating at Tampa Airport, Florida and Seattle Airport, virtually as a

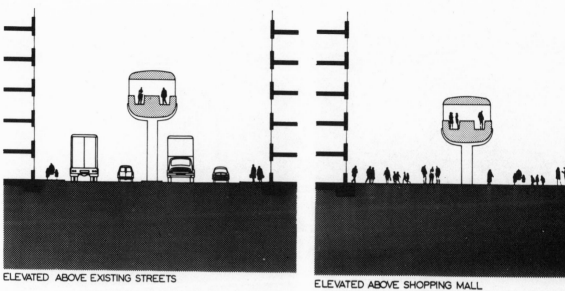

ELEVATED ABOVE EXISTING STREETS

ELEVATED ABOVE SHOPPING MALL

Cross sections showing locations possible of conveyor system in an existing street with or without traffic. In pedestrian street system can be lowered to acceptable clearance for service vehicles, such as fire trucks.

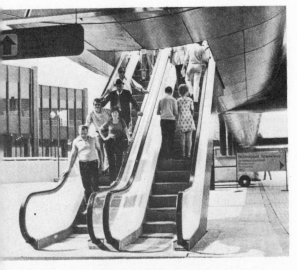

iew of escalators entering elevated pedestrian walkway
stem for Dusseldorf (refer also p. 23).

orizontal lift and a further use would be
ppropriate in a city context as a shuttle system
om transport terminals or car parks located at
he periphery into or across the central area. The
1ost complete installation now operating is the
.irtrans system at Dallas/Fort Worth Airport (see
age 77) one of the first examples of a new complex
ompletely integrated to its own transport system
nd its use here will closely parallel the
equirements of pedestrian movement within an
xisting or new city. The system provides for
,edestrian movement over thirteen miles of one-
'ay track between four passenger terminals, two
arking areas, a hotel and offices and is capable of
xtensions and of carrying mail and refuse and
upplies in containers on special vehicles. (page 44).

'pposite:
*'*erspective showing Speedaway running above existing
,edestrian shopping street, off-centre to allow sunlight to
nter.

The critical problem of insertion of any new system
within an existing street for pedestrians, consisting
of either conveyor or vehicle system and requiring
a segregated track, is simply that the width of the
average city street is rarely above 100 feet and that
an elevated system is ideally located over the
centre of the road where it causes minimal
overshadowing or over-looking to offices or flats on
either side. In this location however, underground
services may require moving to enable column
foundations to be built, which adds considerably
to the cost. The underneath of the track is that
part of the system most visible to the pedestrian
and one-way vehicular systems which halve this
dimension are often proposed for this reason
although two-way systems of movement are
preferable for pedestrians. Stations or boarding
points represent the most serious physical problem
of integration into a city with dimensions up to
200′ long by 90′ wide for a two-way station and
which unless capable of being integrated into new
development may have to be accepted as free-
standing elements in the street, ideally located at
400 yard intervals.

Finding acceptable locations for stations of this
size may govern the actual route of the system and
it may be decided to use a one-way in preference to
a two-way system because of its reduced visual
impact, and in preference to the cost of putting it
underground. A study completed for Denver,
Colorado, in 1972 for the Regional Transportation
District showed one-way systems at the periphery
of the central area primarily because the building
densities were lower here and the stations being
less bulky, were easier to locate. This study is
important in that it shows how the vehicular

31

UNDERGROUND

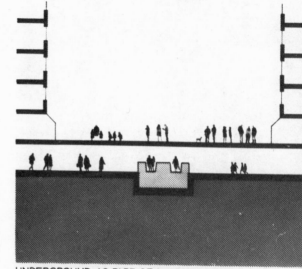

UNDERGROUND AS PART OF SHOPPING MALL

system would be complemented by the other pedestrian movement systems within the CBD, such as the pedestrian mall, the cycle ways, minibus system and possible conveyor system. Where shopping streets have been closed to traffic it may be acceptable to run an elevated pedestrian movement system at low level with sufficient clearance to form a covered arcade below and provide street lighting in the soffit of the track or tube. In the study shown (page 30) the system was placed off-centre above the pedestrian street to avoid overshadowing the sunny side and fire

Above:
Underground locations possible for a conveyor system below an existing street, or pedestrian only system running alone in tunnel or part of an underground shopping concourse connecting into the basements of existing shops. Services represent a significant problem in planning systems underground.

Perspective section, using Speedaway system running in individual city block lengths with pedestrian concourses between.

32

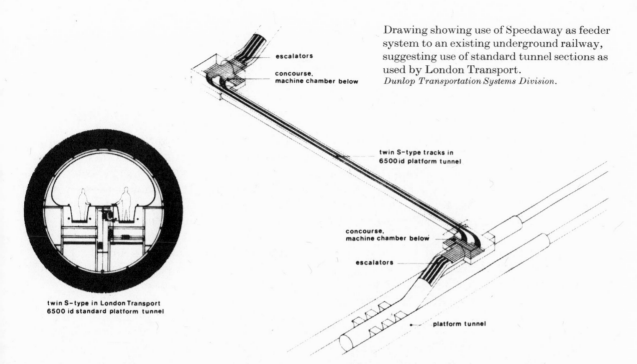

escalators

concourse,
machine chamber below

twin S-type tracks in
6500 id platform tunnel

concourse,
machine chamber below

escalators

platform tunnel

twin S-type in London Transport
6500 id standard platform tunnel

egulations permitted the tube to run twenty feet
6m) from the building frontage. An elevated
onveyor system requires relatively small boarding
oints, and in the Dusseldorf installation (page 31)
scalators are integrated into the underside of the
ube which would be acceptable within a pedestrian
treet at the 400 yard intervals required.

Alternatively, elevated light rail systems such as
he minirail may be acceptable, and certainly the
xperience of the Swiss National Exhibition of
964 showed that a slow-speed (10 mph) small,
ilent system running three metres high over
edestrians added much animation to the scene,
nd the size of a station in a simple system such
s this is half that required by the advanced
ystems (see pages 71–83) which require the off-line
tations.

Studies showing how networks of overhead
ystems could be integrated into existing streets
which still retain the traffic are likely to be hotly

debated by property owners overlooking the
guideways, and their advantages do seem
debatable, the system being an overlay on an
existing situation. Real advantages could only be
obtained when used at a limited number of
strategic points within a city such as from fringe
car parks, bus or rail terminals where they would
carry people to and from the business area and
allow for an overall reduction in traffic. Also their
visual impact on the streets over which they were
run could be lessened if traffic could be reduced or
the street made pedestrian only, so producing an
overall environmental gain. The merits of complete
networks to serve internal movement in existing
cities appear debatable, probably better obtained
by conventional systems, walking or buses, but are
much more practicable in large scale new
developments where they could contribute greatly,
in much the same way as has the development
of the lift or escalator, and either rights of way left
for their installation as and when required, or a
system selected which can be added to in stages.

An interchange can be described as a place where transfer occurs between one or more kinds of transport system and may be of several different kinds:

1. Park and ride interchange
2. Kiss and ride interchange between cars onto bus or rail
3. Bus-rail interchange
4. Pedestrian to rail or bus
5. Interchange between vehicles of the same system, such as bus to bus or rail to rail.

Studies have shown that the travelling public dislike interchanging above all, and that even having to interchange may deter them from using public transport. Today by no means all movement in a city is to and from the centre where public transport networks, which have usually evolved on a radial pattern, can give an adequate service. Future movement is likely to be increasingly directed towards areas outside, which although accessible by car now, as congestion increases, are unlikely to be so in the future, so that access by public transport is likely to involve one or more interchanges. At these points a traveller loses time, both walking or waiting during transfer and London Transport studies on passenger response indicate that activities associated with movement are rated as relatively pleasant, such as riding on an escalator, while waiting, especially in crowded conditions, is rated as unpleasant. In existing situations authorities are often improving waiting conditions by means of better lighting, providing seats and attractive wall finishes with posters to read, and notable work has been done by Cambridge Seven Associates for the Massachusetts

Bay Transportation Authority (MBTA). Walking conditions too at interchanges are freqently improved by providing passenger conveyors as has been done at the Chatelet underground station in Paris, which psychologically reduce walking distances during interchange. At surface level, much can still be done to give priority to the siting of bus stops, at points convenient for travellers interchanging, more easily achieved once bus lanes, or bus-only roads are introduced.

Often quite simple low-cost measures may be undertaken to improve interchange for passengers. For example by the selection of a bus which is easy to get on and off and is large enough to provide seats at peak hour. Or the planning of its route and the system of ticketing so that one ticket can be used on bus and train. Important too is the ease of access from bus to station platform, and the clarity of the signing and scheduling which helps to reduce waiting time during transfer. Studies were completed in 1973 on the effect of introducing these kind of inexpensive improvements at thirteen selected stations in Merseyside involving bus/rail and car/rail interchange with the aim that passenger reaction could first be tested before spending large sums of money.

In new interchanges high standards of design are possible provided the funds are budgeted for at the outset. Good finishes, for example cost more and if carefully selected can reduce maintenance. Interchanges today, try to combine as many modes of transport as possible under one roof and the study for the City of Southampton (opposite) proposes combining an existing long distance coach station now 600 yards away, with a medium-

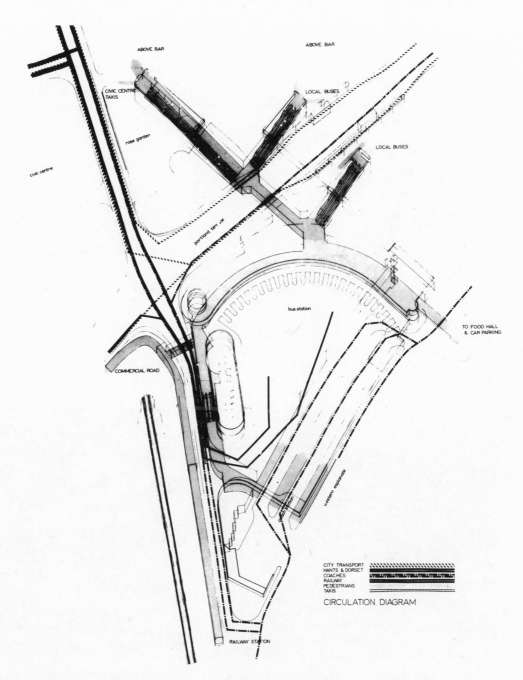

ABOVE BAR

ABOVE BAR

CIVIC CENTRE
TAXIS

LOCAL BUSES

rose garden

LOCAL BUSES

civic centre

portland terrace

bus station

TO FOOD HALL
& CAR PARKING

COMMERCIAL ROAD

western esplanade

CITY TRANSPORT
HANTS & DORSET
COACHES
RAILWAY
PEDESTRIANS
TAXIS

CIRCULATION DIAGRAM

RAILWAY STATION

Study of a new bus-rail interchange for Southampton adjoining the city centre. Connections are shown, using escalators and conveyors between taxis, city buses, medium distance buses and long distance coaches with links to the railway station.

Architect: Brian Richards – Consultant Engineers: Ove Arup.

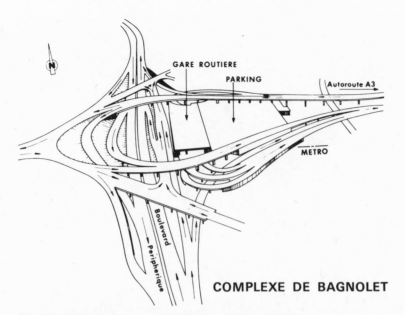

GARE ROUTIERE

PARKING

Autoroute A3

METRO

Boulevard Peripherique

COMPLEXE DE BAGNOLET

Opposite:
Plan and aerial view of 'Kiss and ride' and feeder bus layout at the Finch station on the subway in Toronto. Location of the ticket concourse below street is shown dotted. Up to 100 cars will circulate at one time around the island where passengers wait in the warm to be picked up.
Toronto Transit Commission.

Bus/Car/Rail interchange at Gallieni, on the east of Paris, showing road access for 3 level 2,400 place garage and bus station for 22 buses.

View of bus station with unloading space for 22 single deck buses with escalators and stairs down to concourse below. Cycle storage is provided below for personnel.

View of Gallieni, interchange, station platform. The interchange was made possible by extension of the existing Metro, allowing for two new stations to be built.
Regie Autonome des Transports Parisiens.

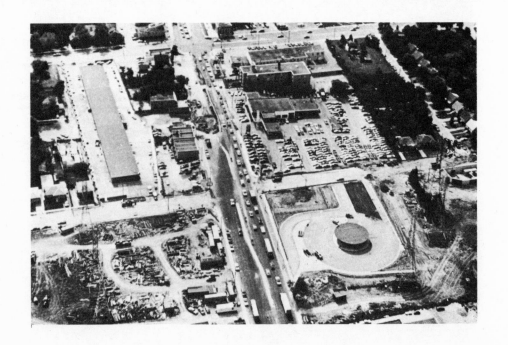

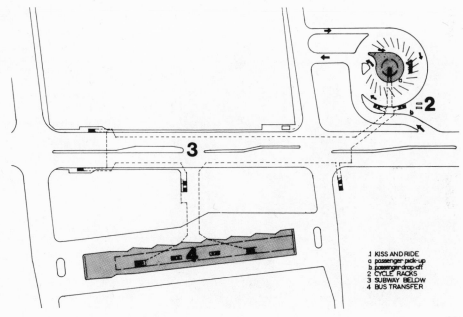

1 KISS AND RIDE
a passenger pick-up
b passenger drop-off
2 CYCLE RACKS
3 SUBWAY BELOW
4 BUS TRANSFER

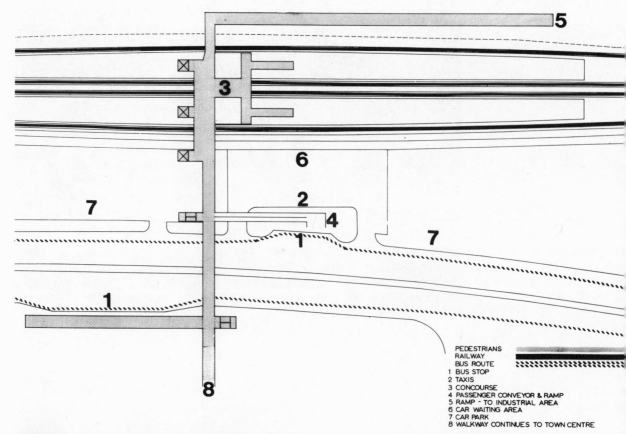

PEDESTRIANS
RAILWAY
BUS ROUTE
1 BUS STOP
2 TAXIS
3 CONCOURSE
4 PASSENGER CONVEYOR & RAMP
5 RAMP - TO INDUSTRIAL AREA
6 CAR WAITING AREA
7 CAR PARK
8 WALKWAY CONTINUES TO TOWN CENTRE

INTERCHANGE STATION AT STEVENAGE

Plan for elevated railway station for Stevenage which
includes an elevated walkway (5) crossing the line,
providing pedestrian access between the Town Centre
and the industrial zone. A conveyor and ramp (4)
connects this to a local bus stop and taxi stand.

View of conveyor and ramp up from taxi and bus stand
at Stevenage station.
Dunlop.

distance bus station and provide interchange with local buses and taxis all under cover. A covered pedestrian link is also proposed connecting with the existing railway station 350 yards away, too costly to move. Planning schemes of this kind are orientated principally towards easing pedestrian movement between different modes and in both this and many interchanges in Germany such as in Munich (pages 17–18) small shops are used along the pedestrian route adding vitality by day and interest at night and which in busy urban areas combined with good pedestrian connections help to integrate the development into the city.

There are situations, however, where an environment may be already committed to handling traffic and the Gallieni station in Paris (page 36) shows a building integrated into the centre of a motorway interchange providing parking for over 2,000 cars and access for express buses directly off the motorway, designed principally for commuters who proceed by Metro at basement level. Here the station has only very tenuous pedestrian linkages into the surrounding community and is designed principally as a mechanism for handling vehicles and people. Many 'park and ride' stations of a simpler kind have similar problems, and with only ground level parking are able to be changed as pressure on land increases. Rarely provided is proper access for pedestrians or cyclists and, what parking there is is often insufficient, frequently spilling over into residential areas. One excellent example of

interchange is shown in the plan of the new Finch Station (page 37) on the Toronto subway where pedestrian access is provided at several points, a cycle park and well-considered buildings for 'kiss and ride' and feeder bus operation. This kind of facility combined with a regular and frequent service must be considered essential in any transport policy aimed at getting people to use public transport. While in planning transport networks the aim should be to eliminate the need for interchange entirely, in practice this occurs when a traveller completes his journey on foot. A well-designed interchange must make walking easy and both eliminate pedestrian/vehicle conflict and provide easy means of changing level, particularly important for the disabled. The plan of Stevenage station (page 38) shows how an elevated pedestrian route (5) which connects the Town Centre with the industrial zone is integrated into the station design crossing both railway and main road at high level and provided with ramps and a pedestrian conveyor (page 38) down to ground level where local bus stops and a taxi rank are situated.

Planning for pedestrian movement at interchange points such as have been described is essentially a micro-scale problem in which satisfactory detailed considerations effect daily large numbers of people passing through. While the service provided by the system is of primary importance ultimately the quality of passenger interchanges must make some contribution to a public's acceptance of public transport.

Any policy aimed at improving the environment of the city must also be directed at finding ways of solving the problem of servicing and deliveries which can account for one fifth and more of vehicles moving on a city's streets. Already many cities are enforcing laws about the size of vehicles which they allow to enter, and where they can be used. Stockholm for example now limits trucks to 12 metres length weighing no more than 3.5 tons to using no more than a very limited network of streets. Others have, due to the growth of pedestrian-only streets enforced not only the time at which vehicles can enter the street but also the weight of the vehicles. Essen for example permits vehicles only to enter the pedestrian street between 7 pm and 10 am, and not to weigh more than 3.5 tons. Many other cities, such as Cologne or Copenhagen provide lay-by spaces off the pedestrian streets for trucks to unload and goods to be trolleyed. Neither systems of delivering goods appears to cause great problems for either shopkeeper, supplier or pedestrian who are content to enjoy the increased trade and environmental benefits from a street which is free of continuously moving vehicles. The objections previously made that shops had to have rear access before streets could be paved, with the exception of those shops like large supermarkets, which generate large numbers of vehicles, do not now appear valid, and often where this has been done the results have not been worth the effort, negating as they do any opportunity of extending the pedestrian area in depth and in historic cities being enormously destructive. Some cities find that basement servicing areas for several adjoining buildings can be combined when redevelopment of an area takes place, and Dallas, Texas, for example

is building a depot of this kind, where large numbers of trucks can be off-loaded. Studies undertaken for Toronto, suggested that as offices accounted for 40% of truck stops in the core area, one way of reducing this would be by providing more storage space. An experiment was made in London 'Operation Moondrop' with a number of selected stores providing late night deliveries and although unpopular due to overtime staff being required is now being revived. Night-time deliveries however are frequently noisy and often objected to by residents.

All the systems discussed above assume that trucks still enter the city, and it seems that if an overall environment improvement of the city is to be made the problem requires a wider scale of approach. The system of siting trucking terminals or depots at the periphery of the city has long been established in New York and could if sufficiently up-graded prove to be probably the most logical method of rationalising the movement of goods in cities. Such terminals, adjoining railways, canals and primary roads could be designed to handle all goods destined for or leaving the city. Computer-controlled warehouses and their mechanical handling equipment are now so efficient that double handling need cost little more and be offset by the advantages of goods being stored and consolidated for delivery economically and when required. The principle would be that of off-loading all goods and vehicles into the terminal which did not conform to the vehicle specification of the city-centre. Goods would then be consolidated according to their appropriate area, and carried by special vehicles in standard containers equipped with built-in unloading and

A

B

Range of electric vehicles used in Zermatt, Switzerland
for different purposes, (a) Hotel (b & c) Builders
(d) Water/beer.

Lousada.

C

D

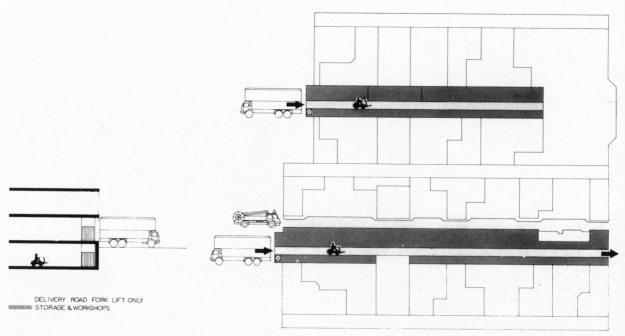

DELIVERY ROAD FORK LIFT ONLY
STORAGE & WORKSHOPS

Basement service area in Free University, Berlin, by
Candilis, Josic, Woods, Schiedhelm, keeps trucks at
ground level at periphery and uses a freight elevator and
electric fork lift truck along corridors 140 metres long.

loading devices. The vehicles would be compact
and non-polluting, possibly battery operated, and
highly manoeuvrable, permitting considerable
economy to be made in the design of the service
area of buildings.

An example of the concept of actually reducing
the scale of service areas by changing the vehicle
size is at the Free University at Berlin where truck
bays are sited at the periphery at ground level and
large goods lifts provided used by electric fork lift
trucks which can off-load and run along the
corridors carrying the goods at basement level to
storage areas.

One working example of a computerised freight
terminal exists at Groningen in Holland, a town
with a population of 150,000 which has a terminal
outside the town used by ninety two hauliers who
share the running costs and rent a bay and storage
area with the use of the terminal's own delivery
vehicles.

An example of the range of vehicles to be found is
seen at Zermatt, Switzerland, where the size of the
village streets and dense pedestrian movement
necessitate the use of small-scale electric vehicles,
designed to suit a wide range of uses. Most
proposals for goods handling in existing cities in
the future stem from the principle that peripheral

42

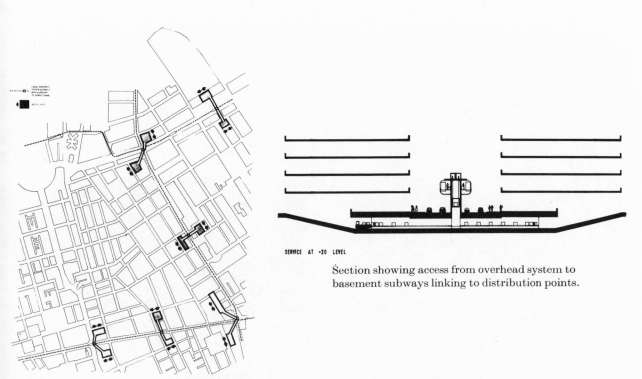

SERVICE AT +20 LEVEL

Section showing access from overhead system to
basement subways linking to distribution points.

Plan showing proposed location of goods distribution
depots for Central London. Goods are carried at off-peak
in containers on overhead system and transfer onto
electric trucks in each zone.
(*Project by B. Richards, 1966*).

goods terminals are provided. In the larger cities
smaller terminals would have to be located closer
to their destination to decrease travel distances
for delivery trucks and new technology could
provide a more efficient method of delivering goods
to these secondary terminals. For example an
automatic vehicular movement system such as the
Airtrans system (page 44) operating at Dallas/
Fort Worth Airport running underground, could
provide transport for people and use special
vehicles at off-peak hours to deliver containers to
local terminals automatically, thence to be
delivered to local destinations by electric truck.
A study for an underground automated container
system by the Canadian Transport Commission

for Ottawa proposed using conveyors to carry the
containers within a five foot diameter underground
pipe to sixty local downtown terminals which
could be a maximum $2\frac{1}{2}$ mile distance from any
'subscriber' to the system.

Pneumatic tube systems are already being widely
used in Russia to carry materials in capsules within
a pipe 1 metre in diameter a distance of 2 km. In
1967 the West German Postal Authorities built a
twin pipeline a distance of 1.8 km. to carry
capsules 1.6 metres long and 0.45 metres in
diameter between the main and sub-Post Office
at speeds of 30 km/hr and the system carries up to
one million letters a day. A pneumatic system,

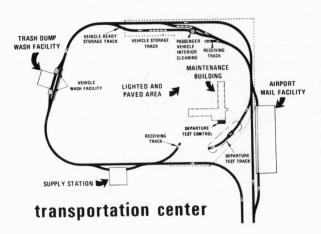

transportation center

Plan of Airtrans Transportation Centre at Dallas/Fort Worth Airport showing location of mail, supplies and waste facilities.

Departure point from the track where vehicles enter after maintenance.

Various container sizes for each type of goods, which are lifted off vehicles at depots or stations automatically.

Standard vehicle chassis designed to carry different containers. *LTV Aerospace Corporation.*

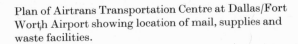

Passenger

Employee

Baggage   Passenger Body

Mail   Utility Body

Supplies

Trash   Common Chassis

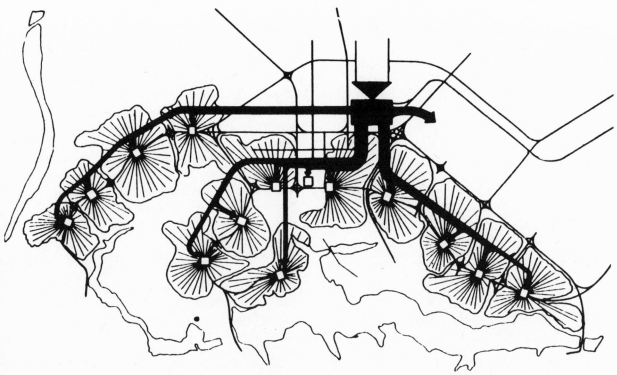

Schematic plan of goods distribution proposed for a new town of 135,000 people at Etarea, Czechoslovakia. Heavy black line indicates route of underground electric trolley routes from main supply centre to district centres. Radiating lines indicate pneumatic tube layout serving homes. *Prague Institute of Architectural Design.*

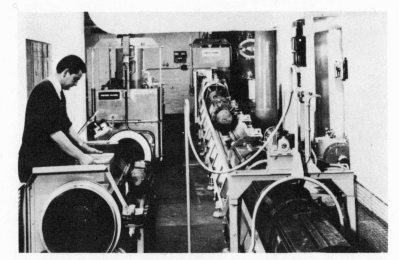

Pneumatic tube systems commissioned in 1967, carrying mail between main and sub-Post Offices in Hamburg, a distance of 1.8 km. View showing 1.6 metre long wheeled containers carrying letters and parcels at speed of 30-36 km/hr.

naturally limits the dimensions of the goods carried but is relatively cheap to introduce and operate with a 3 foot diameter pipeline costing around £100,000 a mile in 1973, which would be less if inserted within shared services ducts.
A pneumatic waste disposal system is already operating in Sundyberg, Sweden serving over 3,000 flats and costing around 1% of the total cost of each flat and an expanded version of this system was studied for a new town for Etarea (page 45), Czechoslovakia intended to serve a population of 135,000. Here the system was intended to deliver goods from district centre warehouses to the home. A scheme of this kind, technically feasible today, combined with cable television for goods selection could in the future be considered as a possible way of reducing the need for vehicular movement, although a simpler method being studied at Chalmers University, Gothenburg, proposes using trailers carrying containers, pulled by buses along busways at off-peak hours which are automatically dropped off into each resident's box at each bus stop to be collected later.

Introducing new methods of handling goods, and deliveries into a city even on an incremental basis requires powerful support from traders and suppliers, still wedded to using trucks of ever-increasing dimensions, and it is likely that they will only be accepted if they can be shown to be reliable, and save time and money compared to conventional delivery systems. This is a field of transport which although much studied requires urgent Government investment into real 'on the ground' experiments.

While serious efforts are being made to improve the pedestrian environment in city centres, comparatively little is being done of a similar kind in existing residential areas. As in the central area, apart from the question of actual distance, the quality of the environment plays an important part in deciding the extent of walking, whether there are shops or items of interest, whether others are walking, or if the pavement is sheltered or windswept. Many areas however have been laid out with little or no regard for the pedestrian and while much effort and money can be focused on improvements within the central area, there are some possible ways of improving the pedestrian environment, for example by eliminating through traffic, by traffic management, landscaping measures such as planting trees or by reducing the extent of barriers to movement by providing street crossings of the primary roads. A possible strategy for the improvement of pedestrian movement systems could be to concentrate first on the points of primary generation of pedestrian traffic, the public transport stops, bus and rail, which together with schools and shops generate the principle flows of people, usually conflicting with existing traffic. The solution may be simply to provide for pedestrian-controlled traffic lights which give adequate time for crossing from any direction or may require more costly means such as well-designed, well-lit subways with escalators to handle the change of level, and containing some small shops as is common in most German cities, with ramps for use by old people.

Street layouts within existing housing areas can be frequently modified at relatively low cost in order that buses can run on more efficient routes to collect or distribute people. For example, short lengths of road may be built to link adjoining housing estates, and fitted with bus-controlled barrier arms which allow buses to pass through without enabling other vehicles to take short cuts. Proper consideration too must be given to the siting of bus stops related to people's actual requirements, near street corners rather than in the centre of a block. New systems of transport could be introduced, now under extensive trial in the U.S. called 'dial-a-ride' (see page 92) which could help to improve mobility in areas where densities are low, or where conventional bus services cannot be run due to the layout. This system requires a high telephone ownership or easy access to one and uses a minibus to pick up people and deliver them door to door or to a number of fixed places such as stations or local shops, not only serving that large section of the population which are without cars but also reducing the need for two car ownership. Personal rapid-transit systems (see page 79) are likely to be introduced into existing residential areas in the future and are intended to have close station spacing and run on dense networks, providing a more useful service than that provided by conventional rapid transit. Ideally each station would be within walking distance of the home, in medium/high density areas and at each station vehicles would be on call, possibly twenty-four hours a day. A combination of this system with dial-a-ride could help to satisfy the latent demand for movement existing in those households which either have limited access to a private car or are without one altogether. Residential development in new towns has to be planned in such a way that

Personal rapid transit stations in residential areas could be reached on foot, cycle, by dial-a-ride bus or by private or hire car. *U.S. Dept. of Housing and Urban Development.*

The first operational Ginkelvan in Vail, Colorado, a new ski resort where it operates on a no-fare basis linking hotels, the centre, and the ski lifts.
Interior view showing angled seating for 15 passengers with standing room. Wide sliding doors and a 7″ step are for ease in boarding and leaving. *Van Ginkel Associates.*

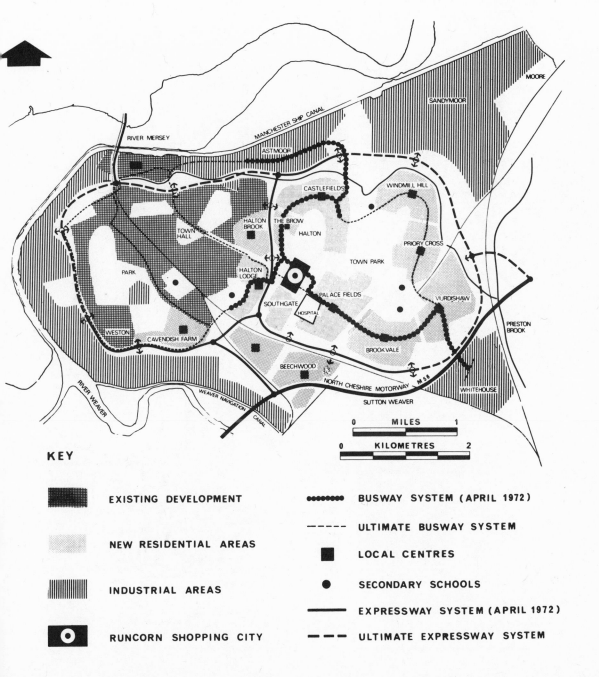

Plan of Runcorn, England, a new town for 70,000 showing the extent of the present and ultimate 12 mile long busway running on a figure of eight loop through the town centre, beside the industrial areas. Bus stops along the route are a maximum 5 minute walk from homes.
Runcorn Development Corporation.

49

Castlefields, Runcorn, a community for over 9,000 people, at an average density of 70 persons to the acre (173 persons per hectare).

50

Plan shows the busway route intersecting the pathway system and running below the local centre.

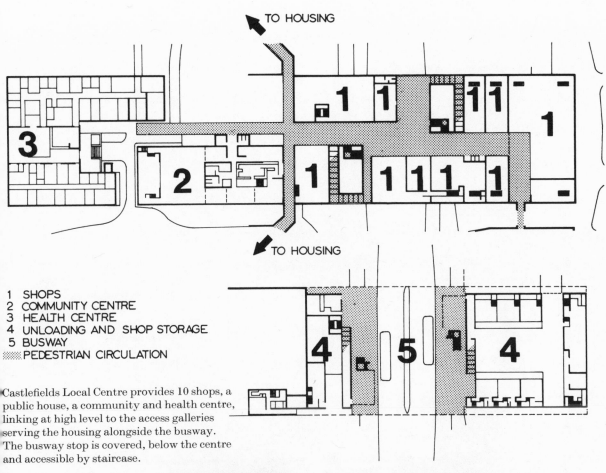

TO HOUSING

TO HOUSING

1 SHOPS
2 COMMUNITY CENTRE
3 HEALTH CENTRE
4 UNLOADING AND SHOP STORAGE
5 BUSWAY
▓▓ PEDESTRIAN CIRCULATION

Castlefields Local Centre provides 10 shops, a
public house, a community and health centre,
linking at high level to the access galleries
serving the housing alongside the busway.
The busway stop is covered, below the centre
and accessible by staircase.

the entire range of transport systems are
considered. Whether building is to be at high or
low density is the most fundamental decision
made, one which affects the capability of
providing for good public transport which is
economic to run or requires a large subsidy. High
densities (which do not mean high building)
usually can provide for better public transport at
lower cost, and bus or rail stops are able to be
located within walking distance of the home. Low
densities are more likely to require a higher degree
of public transport subsidy, and except for dial-a-
ride systems require longer walks from home to
transport stop. Regardless of the density, there are
many possibilities for the layout to be planned as

51

Aerial view of Runcorn Town
Centre, showing the elevated
busway crossing in the foreground.
Buses will run at 5 minute intervals
at off-peak periods, at an average
20 mph and maximum 40 mph.

Covered busway platform in Town
Centre. Stairs give access down to
main shopping level below.
Runcorn Development Corporation.

52

rt of a pedestrian/public transport network
ther than one orientated towards purely private
ansport. Planning which places a high priority on
e needs of the pedestrian or cyclist to visit a
rner shop, or school and allows cars second
ace, are now proving to be popular and those
oviding segregated systems are often safer,
though not essential. Cumbernauld New Town,
otland for example, which has a very complete
twork has one-sixth of the accident rate of any
her new town.

uncorn, England, is perhaps the best example of
new town being planned for 70,000 people,
hich has been designed around a public
ansport system, a bus-only road – twelve miles
ng, which permits the buses to run at an
erating speed of 21 mph, twice the average.
usway stops are situated at a maximum
0 yard walk from all houses and most are closer,
ith local shopping centres situated at busway
ops and often planned to cross the busway
ee page 51). The busway runs on a figure of
ght loop and twelve vehicles will be used at
ff-peak periods which will provide a five minute
eadway, with forty vehicles being used at peak
our. The busway is segregated and runs at high
vel through the city centre but elsewhere runs at
round level, or in cutting, crossing neighbourhood
ads through light-controlled junctions which
ives the buses priority over other vehicles.
lthough a wide variety of alternative systems
as studied in 1964, it is perhaps possible now
at if such systems, as that now operational at
e Dallas/Fort Worth Airport, were available
hen the bus system was selected, (this
re-supposes sufficient funds would have been

forthcoming), they might have been considered for
use in Runcorn. While buses have the considerable
advantage of being added to incrementally, at
low capital cost they are unlikely to provide the
kind of twenty-four hour 'on demand' service
given by automated systems such as these and it
is to be hoped that costs could so be reduced in the
new systems that their use could be brought within
the realms of future new town construction.
Another important aspect of design in Runcorn
is that of road access into some of the housing,
being of pedestrian scale, accepting that such
roads are shared by people and vehicles,
particularly by children close to their homes and
that these must move at slow speeds. Humps in
roads are now commonly used as one way of
slowing vehicles down under these circumstances.
Cycling requires every encouragement in
residential areas, and particularly for provision
for cycles to be made at rapid transit stations, or
bus stops, and for storage to be available for them
at the home at points where they are easily
accessible.

An example of a town designed on the principle of
restricted access by private car is that of Port
Grimaud in the south of France, where adjoining
the Mediterranean houses face on to an artificial
lake on one side and a pedestrian street the other.
Vehicular access to each house, or to the shops
is permitted for dropping or picking up goods by
residents only and this is controlled by providing
two police-manned gateways at the entrance to
the town where all vehicles are stopped and
checked. Visitors cars are excluded entirely and
park with the residents at ground level outside
the gateways, where a total of 1,250 spaces are

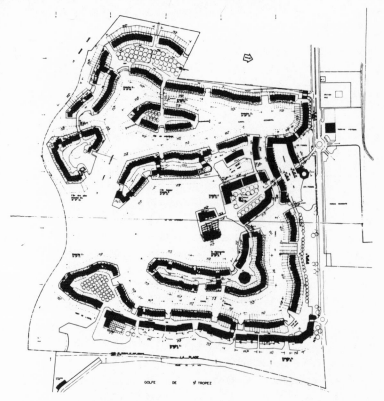

Plan of Port Grimaud, France, first stage shows layout of housing accessible from shared pedestrian/car roadway in centre, opening onto moorings on other side.

Below right:
Entry into Port Grimaud is through two police-controlled gateways. No visitors can drive in, only service vans or residents and short-wait parking is permitted inside.

provided. All movement within the town is on foot or by cycle along the pedestrian streets where due to the density of people, delivery vehicles move cautiously and a free water bus also circulates around the lake at about ten minute intervals stopping at various landing stages. The town, although designed principally for holiday use and wealthy people, does provide for relatively cheap housing and greatly reduces the area of land given over to roads and garages. This is an experiment which could usefully be considered as a principle for housing those people who do not want to own cars or are prepared to live away from them.

It is only fair to say that in spite of the apparent success of the first stage of this development, Stages 2 and 3 will provide parking adjoining the homes. Other ways are being tried in planned communities in Florida and Arizona to deal with the car by planning peripheral roads serving the homes, permitting the use of golf carts on the Radburn-type walkway system which is shared by pedestrians and cyclists and gives access to shops without crossing the main roads.

Parking for 1,200 cars is outside residential area, for visitors and residents who then enter on foot through gateway on right.

population growth, longer holidays and a shorter working week combined with higher wages are all factors contributing to a demand for more leisure activities. Getting to 'places for leisure', has become increasingly easy for car owners with the construction of rural motorways but it is likely in the future that intensive Government finance will be required to plan properly for recreation, particularly in the country, if the very amenity people have come to enjoy is not destroyed.

Local Accessibility: The provision of more leisure facilities locally combined with decent homes, can contribute to a reduced need for people to flee outside the cities at weekends. More small parks and playgrounds can be provided within walking and cycling distance of homes and workplaces. For example in New York City the decision to close Central Park to cars at weekends resulted in more than 10,000 cyclists using it in a single day. Swimming pools and sports centres (many small ones are better than few of Olympic scale) require to be sited where they are accessible to residents and workers on foot or by cycle, close to rail or bus routes. These means of improving accessibility to leisure facilities by public transport will allow them to be easily enjoyed by a non-car owning population and those without access to a car.

Countryside accessibility: Present planning policies for recreation in the country assume, not without justification that those people with cars will want to use them, but that strict controls must be made in selected areas. Experiments at Peak Park's Goyt Valley in England, which was closed to traffic, showed that people would accept leaving their cars at peripheral points and walking or riding a minibus. Yosemite National Park in California, has refused to widen existing roads and offers free shuttle buses from the car parks with cycle hire and horse-riding as alternatives to driving.

Access to the country at week-ends by public transport is however limited and can never hope to be as convenient for families with children as taking a car. The principal factor is the seasonal nature of the demand and unpredictability of climate in many countries, so that heavy subsidies would be required if year-round services were to be run with the same standard of service, although private coach-tour operators fill an important need here. The car hire market too, offers at least for drivers, an alternative either for all-day hire, assuming fuel costs remain reasonable, or for short-term use (see pages 96–97) where a cheaply hired electric vehicle would be available at any railway, bus or coach station for driving the family to the nearest park. Another alternative is for trailer buses to be used, capable of carrying from 20 to 150 people, depending on demand and running to and from the nearest public transport stops.

Long vacation accessibility: The transport requirements of people on holiday naturally varies between those who prefer the crowded beach to the mountain top and it is in the densely used areas that the real problems exist. Mass holidays are generally easily made in European countries by bus, rail and air as well as by private car but it is this last system which causes the biggest environmental problem at the large resorts. Were short-term hire, battery operated minicars

55

Litchfield Park, Arizona with an eventual population of 75,000 planned with grade separated pathways, to take pedestrians, bicycles and electric golf carts. These have a maximum speed of 15 mph and are suitable for short trips. *Neil Koppes.*

Opposite:
Transportation Centre at Walt Disney World, Florida showing park-and-ride facilities, parking for 12,000 cars on left, park for 120 buses in foreground and transport for visitors by choice of steamboat, monorail, or road tram. *Walt Disney Productions.*

available (pages 96–97) combined with good public transport and cycle and moped hire, stiffer restraint measures on car penetration could be made, greatly improving the present conditions. In the towns and cities visited by tourists, traffic is already so dense that special measures of restraint have to be imposed during the season, and some Italian towns like Urbino now adopt these measures on a permanent basis. Salzburg for example limits the number of cars entering the town before closing the gates, and smaller ones like Polperro, Cornwall provide car parks outside the town for visitors, admitting only residents. In Zermatt, Switzerland the citizens deliberately chose to limit access up to the village, using the existing railway rather than build a road and so maintain the streets for pedestrians only,

and by electric carts or horse-drawn sleighs. In new developments such as holiday villages similar measures can be used, enabling people to stroll with their children in areas safe and free from pollution, also reducing the capital cost of building and maintaining roads and using land economically (see Port Grimaud page 54). Yet few authorities or planners will believe that large scale vehicle-free zones would be accepted by the public and the example of Disney World, Florida, is one of the first examples of this kind of planning which should be visited by anyone involved in planning for leisure on a large scale. Here within an area of 27,000 acres, movement by car is strictly limited and those people who have driven there, leave their cars in the 12,000 space park at the periphery (still too small on busy days)

r leave their buses, continuing by monorail, addle steamer or tram to visit restaurants, shops n the amusement park, a pedestrian-only rea, around half a mile square, serviced from elow and visited by often 40,000 people in a day n foot, walking distances they would rarely onsider doing in their own hometowns.

Large scale planning for leisure of this kind will increasingly be required in certain carefully selected areas in the future if the present pressure on the now limited number of 'places to go' are to be reduced.

57

Mobility represents an important factor in present day living and although the myth persists that this must mean car ownership, the more enlightened city authorities now recognise that to rebuild existing urban areas solely for mass use by cars is both too costly and ludicrous in its inability to keep up with demand.

Added to this is the realisation that not only are one-car families not truly mobile but that often 50% of any country's population are without access to a car. The alternatives of planning around public transport and providing for it must be accepted as the only possible solution and the wide range of systems discussed below indicate what is available today, what is being done, and what can be done in the future.

Moving Pavements
Possibly no city centre system of movement has so captured the minds of inventors in the early part of the century nor of the public than the idea of a moving pavement. All the early systems proposed and built accepted that around 10 mph was a reasonable speed for travel over short distances and solutions were then found to the problem of boarding a platform moving at that speed. The first known moving pavement was proposed for New York in 1874 (see page 59) and was to be an elevated system of articulated platforms running on wheels moving at 15 mph boarded from a number of 6-seat trolleys running parallel with the platforms, which by means of a friction brake could be used for transfer. In 1887, Henard, a planner engaged in a competition for new ideas for the 1889 Exposition in Paris, suggested that continuously moving platforms should be used running at two speeds. The

previous year a three-speed system had been proposed by Rettig which was to run in a subway and consist of parallel platforms moving at 3, 6 and 9 mph, with seats on the fastest platform. Up to this date nothing had actually been built until in 1893 at the Columbian Exhibition in Chicago a two-speed system was designed by Schmidt an engineer and Silsbee an architect which ran in a great ellipse 1,310 metres long and which used twin platforms moving at 3 and 6 mph (see page 59). A subsequent proposal was made for a similar system to be elevated over either side of a Chicago main street at first floor level against the building face with access into the buildings.

In 1894 two French engineers proposed a scheme for parallel underground moving platforms for Paris accessible from ground level by escalator. They considered this is a possible transport solution for Paris, a continuously moving system to be called 'Labyrinthe Parisien' and two years later in 1896 a two-speed platform system 460 m. long was built in Berlin to connect an exhibition ground with a pleasure park. At the same time research and development was being done in Paris for use in the forthcoming exhibition and a competition held by the Administration for a system to encircle the grounds was won in 1898 by three engineers who finally combined their ideas and built a test track using two parallel platforms which ran at speeds of about 3.6 km/h and 7.2 km/h (see page 61). In 1900 this system was installed and operated at the Paris Exhibition on an elevated structure 3.4 km long with nine stations equally spaced along the route and linked by a pavement which ran parallel to the moving platforms. The system ran for eight months, twelve hours a day and was used by $6\frac{1}{2}$ million

58

Proposal for elevated moving pavement for New York, 1874 by Speer.

Detail showing 6-seat car being used as an interchange vehicle to leave the 15 mph system.
L'illustration 1874.

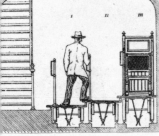

Underground moving platform proposed for Paris in 1888 by Rettig. Platforms to move at 3, 6 and 9 mph.

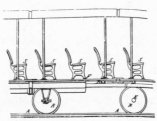

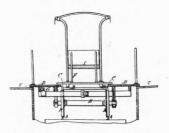

First moving platform system built at Columbian Exposition in Chicago 1893. Platforms moved at 3 and 6 mph.
Scientific American.

people, an average of 120,000 people a day with a total of forty minor accidents. A Pathe newsreel film shows how easily people were able to pass between the platforms moving at two speeds and it became so popular that seats were placed on the faster platforms. It was a great success with the public and writers of the period, H. G. Wells among them regarded it as a 'promise of things to come'. Also operating at the Exhibition were a number of inclined moving ramps, the forerunner of to-day's pedestrian conveyors and escalators. In 1903 Max Schmidt of New York, who had been one of the designers of the Chicago scheme, was awarded the Franklin Institute award 'for improvements made with and used for bringing moving platforms into daily use as a means of transportation in large cities'. In 1904 a scheme was proposed by several leading railway engineers to build a moving platform system to run in a subway below 34th Street in New York with a loop at each end using 4 parallel platforms one of which was to remain stationary for use at off peak time, the others to run at 3, 6 and 9 mile/hour, and although the scheme was never built, it was revived twenty years later. In 1920 the City of Paris held a competition for a transit system to replace the Metro which was won by three engineers, two French, one British. The former proposed to run a continuously moving platform in tunnel at a speed of 10 mph (see page 62) on which were to be seats boarded at stations by an accelerating device capable of moving a passenger from a boarding speed of $1\frac{1}{2}$ mph up to 10 mph or decelerate him when leaving in a distance of ten feet. Full scale tests (page 62) showed that in practice a length of thirty yards would be necessary for people to

60

remain standing, so requiring longer stations and the system was never installed. In 1923 the New York proposals for 42nd Street were again revived by H. S. Putman to run between Times Square and Grand Central Station and a test track was built with three parallel moving platforms driven below by a linear induction motor (page 62) with an estimated capacity of 32,000 seated passengers an hour in each direction. There are varied reports as to why it was rejected, one being that the authorities objected to building a shallow cross-town subway that would make future subway construction impossible.

In the 1930's several other proposals, which were never realised, were made for installing conveyors for the Chicago World's Fair of 1933, and by the architects of Rockefeller Center interested in linking the Center with Grand Central Station. In 1935 a Westinghouse engineer, Storer, designed a subway system called Biway which used an express platform with seats moving at a constant speed of 24 km/h to be boarded from a local platform which was either stationary or accelerated to the speed of the express. Automatic gates between platforms were to open when identical speeds were reached. This system would virtually have eliminated waiting and was to have a potential capacity of 60,000 passengers an hour. A pedestrian conveyor system was used at New York World's Fair in 1939 for people to board small cars for viewing an exhibit and in 1964 a similar design was adopted, and many other systems of this kind are today in use at Disney World, in Florida. Pedestrian conveyors are now used throughout the world at airports and rapid-transit stations and run at between

...t the Paris Exhibition 1900, showing people travelling
...n the two speed moving pavements.
...nprimerie Nationale.

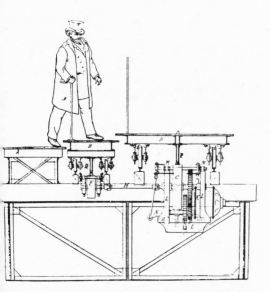

...ection showing flexible continuous steel rail below
...entre of two platforms, driven at intervals by electric
...notors at speeds of 3.6 km/h and 7.2 km/h.

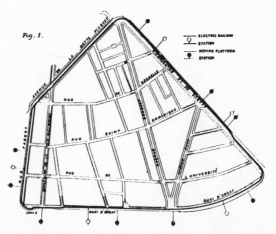

Fig. 1.

Site plan of Paris Exhibition 1900 showing stations for
moving platforms with elevated track 2½ miles long.
Engineering.

61

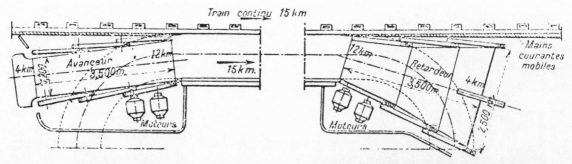

Project for new transport system for Paris 1924.
Platforms to move continuously in tunnel at 10 mph and
conveyor system at station used to accelerate passengers
entering, decelerate for leaving.

Test track for interlocking belts for advancing or
retarding speed.
Centre Nationale de la Recherche Scientifique.

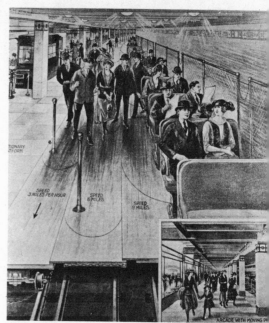

Moving platform system for 42nd Street, New York
1924 with three platforms moving at 3, 6 and 9 mph
Capacity to be 32,000 seated passengers an hour.
Scientific American.

Section through test track of New York proposal showing
linear induction drive.
Scientific American.

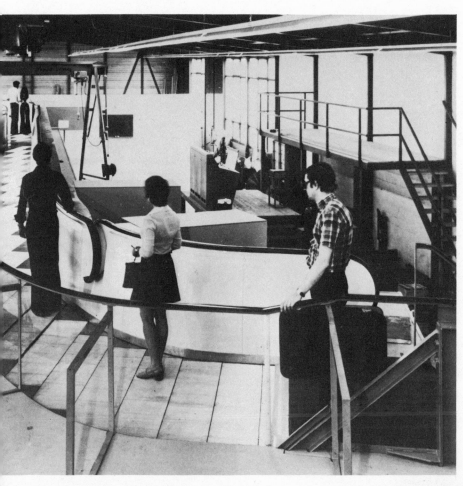

View of Speedaway prototype at Battelle Institute,
Geneva, showing people entering at right and being
accelerated to 3½ times the entry speed.
Dunlop Transportation Systems Division.

Tests being undertaken at Royal Aircraft Establishment,
Farnborough, showing people transferring between a
stationary platform and one moving at 2 km/hr.
carrying assorted luggage.
RAE Farnborough.

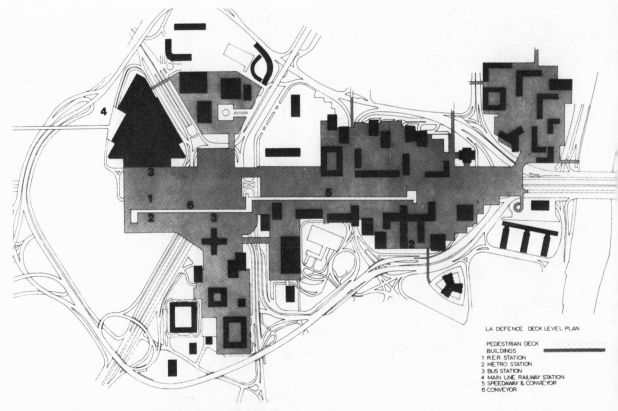

LA DEFENCE DECK LEVEL PLAN

PEDESTRIAN DECK
BUILDINGS
1 R.E.R. STATION
2 METRO STATION
3 BUS STATION
4 MAIN LINE RAILWAY STATION
5 SPEEDAWAY & CONVEYOR
6 CONVEYOR

La Defense, Paris, a new development comprising offices for 100,000 people, homes for 24,000 and a regional shopping centre. Access is by high-speed metro RER (1) local metro (2) buses (3) main line railway (4) car and taxi.

The pedestrian deck covers a motorway and a proposed system for pedestrian movement will run above the deck.

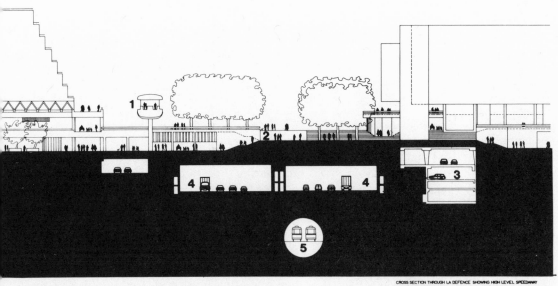

CROSS SECTION THROUGH LA DEFENCE SHOWING HIGH LEVEL SPEEDAWAY

1 SPEEDAWAY & CONVEYOR SYSTEM
2 PEDESTRIAN DECK
3 CAR PARKING
4 MOTORWAY
5 RAPID RAIL

Section showing the relation of the tube (1) carrying pedestrian conveyors to the deck. (2) The motorways (4) and express metro (5) run below the landscaped deck.

Below opposite:
Interior view from within tube. A low lighting level is intended to give good views at night over the floodlit gardens and the pedestrian deck.

Photo of model of La Defense showing location of one section of pedestrian conveyor system and two stations.

2–3 km/h governed by Safety Codes which accepts this as a safe speed to step on or off at either end. This speed, about half normal walking speed, is still useful psychologically provided it is possible to walk on the conveyor, over distances of several hundred feet. For the longer distances of 400 yards and over, there has in the last ten years been active research into accelerating conveyors.

One system proposed in 1964 by Bouladon and Zuppiger of the Institut Battelle in Geneva used a series of platforms boarded like an escalator with sidewalls and doors at front and back which converted into cabins as they accelerated, to the speed of a continuously moving platform alongside. The principle of using an accelerator and decelerator to board or leave a continuously moving platform has been described above (for Paris in 1923) and was in 1971 the subject of a years intensive human engineering study under A. Browning of the Royal Aircraft Establishment, Farnborough, in Britain (page 63).

65

Transfer times of seven to eight seconds were
assessed as being reasonable for the general
public to pass between adjacent platforms and
these experiments and others have helped to
define many critical human engineering factors.
Subsequent work by the Battelle Institute and
Dunlop has led to development of the S-type
Speedaway (page 63) in which passengers are not
required to transfer, simply riding the length of
the conveyor, accelerating on entering and
decelerating on leaving. The platforms look like
an escalator platform but slide relative to one
another as they move forward in a parabolic path.

This system has been running since 1970 as a full
scale test track and has been used in detailed
studies undertaken for La Defense, a new centre
in Paris by the French Authority EPAD. Here it
was proposed to run a 460 metre long Speedaway
in a glazed air-conditioned tube 4 metres above the
pedestrian deck to carry office workers to and
from the express Metro and bus station.

There are many situations in existing cities which
require a system to turn through a radius of
around fifty feet, and once the safety aspects of
transfer from one moving platform onto another
can be solved, and the platforms articulated to
turn, it can be equipped with seats and several
proposals have been made, as well as those by the
Battelle Institute, to board a belt or platform.
In 1966 Ayres and McKenna two American
engineers, devised a type of continuous
accelerator using a 'fishnet' type of composite
material capable of stretching in two ways
simulating the flow of a river between banks, and
used to board a parallel platform. More recent
studies of the system envisage a mesh made up of
aluminium strips like a honeycomb driven below
by a linear motor. An in-line accelerating walkway
has in 1972 been developed by Avery at John
Hopkins University and the full scale prototype
now operating consists of overlapping leaves or
plates that are tilted and slide over one another
as they accelerate or decelerate to a speed of
5 mph. The leaves are closely spaced at the entry
portion forming a continuous flat surface and
form a slightly corrugated surface in the
acceleration section. An important factor in this
type of system which reduces surface area will be
the public's acceptance to stand still when
accelerated to avoid 'bunching' as they decelerate.

It seems certain that high speed conveyors could
make an important contribution to a city
transport system by serving dense corridors of
movement. Although costly, twice the cost of the
conventional conveyors, their higher speeds do
justify this. Their integration into existing streets
if run elevated should be environmentally
acceptable (see pages 30–31) or where they are not,
they might be put underground. Above all,
conveyors are a system which can be expanded in
stages, as funds permit.

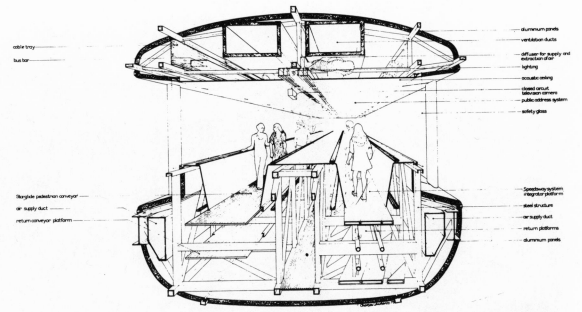

cable tray
bus bar

aluminium panels
ventilation ducts
diffuser for supply and
extraction of air
lighting
acoustic ceiling
closed circuit
television camera
public address system
safety glass

Starglide pedestrian conveyor
air supply duct
return conveyor platform

Speedway system
integrator platform
steel structure
air supply duct
return platforms
aluminium panels

67

Continuous transit system for New
York driven by variable pitch
Archimedean screw. Project by
Adkins and Lewis 1905.
Scientific American.

Wembley Exhibition 1924 showing Never-Stop Railway
cars being turned automatically at end of track.
Railway Gazette.

Car-lator system in Lake Biwa, Japan. Two-seat cars
running at 8 mph give capacity of 3,000 people an hour in
each direction.
Nippon Conveyor Company.

hese systems are capable of carrying up to
),000 people an hour, use small cabins, boarded
hile in motion and capable of turning through a
ght radius, and are suitable as aids to pedestrian
ovement over distances of up to two miles.
1 1905 two British engineers, Adkins and Lewis
roposed a scheme for New York (opposite)
sing small cars running in a tunnel propelled by a
ariable-pitch Archimedean screw, bunching the
rs at boarding platforms they would pass at
mph and accelerating then to 15 mph between
ations. The system was first built in 1923 at
outhend and subsequently ran for two years at
e Wembley Exhibition (1924–5) London, where
carried two million people without accident.
1 1953 Stephens Adamson and Goodyear
onstructed a test unit for a 'Carveyor' system
esigned to replace the 42nd shuttle service in
Ianhattan which used a series of cabins travelling
t 15 mph between stations propelled by a belt,
owing to $1\frac{1}{2}$ mph at stations where boarding
as done from a passenger conveyor running
arallel. The tests showed the system to be
orkable and depending on cabin size capable of
arrying from 5–11,000 people an hour seated.
ecent 'Carveyor' development intends to use a
able drive and the same principle of boarding as
efore and the Poma 2,000 system under trial in
renoble, France has a similar propulsion system.

1 1964 Habegger installed the *telecanape* at the
wiss Exhibition in Lausanne to carry 8,000
eople an hour in each direction over
hree-quarters of a mile from near a railway
tation to the centre of the exhibition. Revolving
0 foot diameter boarding platforms were entered
rom the centre, people walking to the periphery

Test track of Carveyor system showing people stepping
from cabins onto conveyor.

Carveyor system shown superimposed on existing street.
Cars shown bunched are loading and unloading.
Goodyear Transport Systems.

Vec systems showing two person cabins moving at
.3 m/sec. to allow disembarking at stations.
Savec.

Variable speed conveyor using system of overlapping
plates. Plates are closely overlapped at boarding speed,
gradually extending during acceleration.
Applied Science Laboratory John Hopkins University.

(a) Step-on speed

(b) Acceleration

(c) Full speed

Overlapping Leaf Geometry

and boarding the seats passing at around 4 mph.
A similar boarding system is used on the
'Peoplemover' systems at both Disneyland and
Disney World (page 57). The 'Vec' system
developed in France by Cytec (page 70) with a
capacity of 1,000–1,500 people an hour, uses
two-person cabins which slow down at stations
for loading (.3M/Sec) and accelerate using linear
drive between stations (5 M/Sec). A test track has
already carried 70,000 people over a distance of
170 metres, and the first installation will link a
department store with an adjacent car park in
Paris.

range of rail systems are operating to-day or
re under trial at speeds of from 300 mph to
0 mph intended to serve travel needs ranging
om long distance inter-city to short distance
movement within cities.

High speed
The Tokaido Express, runs at a speed of 120 mph
t half hourly intervals within a dense urban
orridor in Japan, over 300 miles long, already
erved by local and express rail systems running
arallel. This service is already over-used and a
much faster system is now being considered.
imilar experiments with high-speed rail have
roved successful between New York and
Washington and developments in the U.K. of the
ew 120 mph APT train designed to run at high
peeds on existing track could extend a demand
or this kind of service on routes where travel
imes by rail are faster than by air and more
onvenient.

Rapid Transit
These systems have long operated in the major
ities throughout the world and are of high
apacity, carrying up to 40,000 passengers or more
n hour in each direction, and suitable for use in
igh density corridors which in the past have
rown up around the system. Today many cities
re considering building extensive rapid transit
etworks and Washington D.C. will, by 1976, have
 24 mile system and extensive use will be made
f Park and Ride facilities at the peripheral
tations and the use of feeder bus systems. Rapid
ransit has the chief advantage of being capable of
unning at high speeds of up to 70 mph on
egregated tracks which with station stops 1–2

miles apart can give an average travel speed of
25–35 mph. Tracks may be situated at various
levels outside the city and normally run
underground within a central area either in deep
or shallow tunnel. The shallow subway, as used
in Montreal or in Paris, has the advantage of
being quickly accessible by pedestrians using it
for short-distance movement of 1–2 miles.
Stations too have the capability of being
integrated with underground shopping streets, as
achieved at Montreal's Place Ville Marie. A new
rapid transit system for a city is extremely costly,
Washington's system is estimated to cost £675
million and many cities are obliged to consider
more economic methods than building completely
new rights of way. Newcastle-upon-Tyne for
example is building a £65 million system
34 miles long which uses 26 miles of existing
railway-track, with a new tunnel across the city
centre, and this will provide a useful system,
closely integrated with the bus system using new
trains and new stations at relatively low cost.

Tramways
These have long been operating successfully in
cities in Europe and the United States and use
electrically driven cars and normally overhead
power lines with a capacity of up to 22,000
passengers an hour in each direction, provided they
can run on segregated tracks. This capacity, half
that of conventional rapid transit and their rapid
acceleration, makes close station spacing economic
(at 1,000 metre intervals) and their use ideal within
medium density corridors. Within central areas,
stops can be at 3–400 metre intervals and the cars
are often run at ground level effectively, provided
they are given priority over other traffic. Traffic

Gothenburg, Sweden, showing junction between zones, and vehicles turning at barriers while trams pass straight through. *Goteborgs Sparvagar.*

management techniques (see pages 10–11) such as those described for Gothenburg or involving the exclusion of all other traffic from the streets, as is done in Amsterdam by widening pavements, can do much to ensure trams are given priority and pedestrian streets may have trams running through them, as in Bremen. Where cities have not been prepared to find road space for trams to run efficiently, the expensive yet environmentally preferable solution may be to build subways, as in Brussels, allowing for the tramway to be converted into a rapid transit system at a future date.

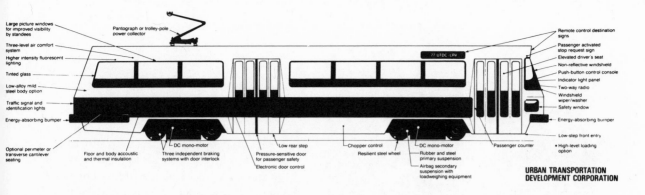

Large picture windows for improved visibility by standees
Three-level air comfort system
Higher intensity fluorescent lighting
Tinted glass
Low-alloy mild steel body option
Traffic signal and identification lights
Energy-absorbing bumper
Optional perimeter or transverse cantilever seating

Pantograph or trolley-pole power collector

77 UTDC - LRV

Remote control destination signs
Passenger activated stop request sign
Elevated driver's seat
Non-reflective windshield
Push-button control console
Indicator light panel
Two-way radio
Windshield wiper/washer
Safety window
Energy-absorbing bumper
Low-step front entry
• High-level loading option

Floor and body accoustic and thermal insulation
DC mono-motor
Three independent braking systems with door interlock
Low rear step
Pressure-sensitive door for passenger safety
Electronic door control
Chopper control
Resilient steel wheel
DC mono-motor
Rubber and steel primary suspension
Airbag secondary suspension with loadweighing equipment
Passenger counter

URBAN TRANSPORTATION
DEVELOPMENT CORPORATION

New design for a tram (the Canadian Light Rail Vehicle
CLRV) produced by the Urban Transportation
Development Corporation, Toronto.

In Brussels a subway has now been built in stages
of sufficient cross section to take trams previously
running at ground level. These will be replaced by
a full-size metro train with four times the
capacity (32,000 passengers an hour). Such a
pre-metro system (see page 74) required low
station platforms to allow for access to the tram
steps later raised to serve the metro floor level.
One of the advantages of this two-stage
pre-metro – metro system in a city already
running trams is that the tunnels and stations can
be used in stages as they are completed by
providing temporary ramps from ground level
down to tunnel level (see diagram) and so
maximise their use during the lengthy and very
high cost construction period. However it is
important to minimise the disadvantages of
placing a surface level transport system which is
so accessible and convenient for travel over short
distances in a city centre. Escalators are necessary
from street to platform level via the mezzanine
in both directions as well as stairs with lifts for the
aged and infirmed and these are far too often
eliminated for reasons of cost or space. Placing
trams underground must be regarded too as a
means of improving the environment of the street,

as Munich has achieved, and allows for pavements
to be widened, trees planted or streets paved over,
not providing space for more vehicles.

San Francisco now uses their trams to complement
the new BART metro and has built stations in
the city centre to provide easy interchange
between both systems, while other cities such as
Boston or Zurich use trams as the principal public
transport mode. Segregation from other traffic
will usually result in higher speeds, although this
may be of marginal advantage in a city centre
where stops are close together. As station spacing
is increased in order to achieve higher speeds in
suburban areas so too may the convenience of
the system decrease. This is particularly critical in
planning new areas of high/medium high density
where car ownership is low. Here stations should
be planned within easy walking distance of all
houses so avoiding the need for feeder buses.

Trams, such as those now being developed for use
in Toronto are now vehicles with a high
acceleration rate (0-30 mph in 12 seconds), and
a low noise level and good suspension and are
now seen by many authorities to have increasing
potential.

Val system being developed for use at a new town, Lille-Est in Northern France. Cabins which run singly or in pairs are 13 metres long 2 metres wide and carry 33 to 37 seated passengers with 16 standing.

These use driverless, rubber-tyred vehicles which carry 15–70 people and run separately or in trains under automatic control stopping at stations as programmed by central computer. The system being driverless must be segregated, elevated, at ground level or underground and is intended to be more economic to run and build than a conventional rapid-transit system. Matra's Val system being developed in France will run on elevated tracks as an automatic shuttle system within a new town, Lille-Est, and connect it with the existing city.

Monorails have similar operating characteristics to Val except that different track and cabin cross sections (see page 103) are used. A system running successfully at Wuppertal, Germany since 1900 has cabins slung below the supporting track. The

Central control system which monitors the location of each Val cabin, shown here at the test track installed at Lille.
Engins Matra.

alternative, originally manufactured by Alweg has cabins astride a single concrete beam and operates at Seattle, Washington and Disneyworld, Florida (see page 57). The reduced scale of the supporting track is especially important visually where the system is to run above street level.

The Minirail Habegger system was first designed for the Swiss Exhibition in Lausanne in 1964 where it ran through many of the pavilions and for Montreal's Expo where it is still running. Using six or eight person cabins linked into trains running automatically on an elevated steel track the system can carry 4-10,000 persons in an hour in each direction at speeds of up to 40 mph. As well as being in use in several fairgrounds and zoos, studies have been completed for an installation at Rimini, Italy, where it is intended to serve summer visitors and be used as part of the city's transport system.

Group-rapid transit (G.R.T.)

This system is basically designed to serve medium-density corridors of movement where conventional rapid-transit is of too high a capacity and cost to justify installation. Group-rapid transit uses off-line stations into which 10–40 passenger, driverless cabins can be switched either as programmed or as individually required. Cabins stop, allowing others to pass on the main tube, (Skip-stop operation) and capacity of the system depends on the headways possible and some manufacturers expect a four second headway to enable 20,000 passengers to be carried an hour in each direction in thirty passenger cabins. Guideways can be elevated, at grade, in cutting or below ground but need to be fully segregated. The Boeing system, (page 76) uses twenty-one person cars operating at 30 mph. at a university campus at Morgantown, West Virginia, and is designed to carry up to 5,000 people an hour in each direction in this first demonstration project funded by the U.S. Government. The system runs on a three mile long guideway both elevated and at ground level, and is intended to be used by the 1,100 students now carried about the campus by seventeen buses. The Airtrans system, built by Ling-Temco-Vought is operating at the new Dallas/Fort Worth airport and uses 42 passenger vehicles operating at 17 mph on a thirteen mile long guideway running elevated and at ground level. It is capable of carrying 9,000 people an hour, between the various airport terminals, the hotel and car parking and special off-line stations and vehicles are used to handle mail, refuse or goods. This is the first example of a new building complex which is integrated completely and relies on a new system of transport technology. The ACT system developed by the Ford Motor Company uses thirty passenger cabins and was one system exhibited at 'Transpo' Washington in 1972 where a 750 foot long guideway, with two stations was used by 25,000 visitors. The system has been selected for use at Bradley International Airport, Connecticut, to run as a shuttle or on demand system on a single three-quarter mile guideway between car park, hotel and airport terminal, with an intermediate bypass allowing two vehicles to be operated.

Minirail crossing parkland at Lausanne.

To the right:
Boeing car climbing a 10 per cent grade on the $2\frac{1}{4}$ miles of guideway at Morgantown, West Virginia, linking the CBD to the university campus.

Plan shows steering and switching system developed by Alden Self-Transit which is controlled from within the car via commands received from the central communication and control system.
The Boeing Company Surface Transportation.

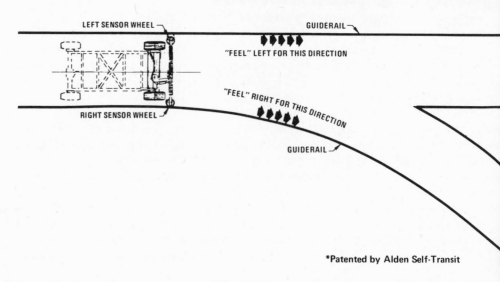

LEFT SENSOR WHEEL — GUIDERAIL —

"FEEL" LEFT FOR THIS DIRECTION

"FEEL" RIGHT FOR THIS DIRECTION

RIGHT SENSOR WHEEL

GUIDERAIL

*Patented by Alden Self-Transit

Airtrans system operating at Dallas/Fort Worth airport. Showing 40 passenger vehicles leaving a terminal building.

Central control console from which the 13 mile long system with 42 vehicles are supervised. Here the automatic operation of the system can be watched, and the status of each vehicle recorded on the route map. T.V. screens permit all stations to be viewed and two-way communications with all vehicles is possible.
Ground Transportation Division, LTV Aerospace Corp.

The TTI Otis personal rapid transit system uses 6 or 10 seat cars driven by linear induction motor and suspended on air bearings. Speeds of up to 30 mph are possible.

Cabins have bi-parting elevator type doors and the air cushion suspension permits cabins to dock sideways into station platforms, to allow others to pass and reduce station size. (*opposite page*). *TTI-OTIS.*

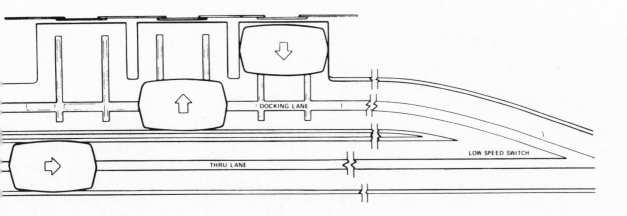

Personal Rapid Transit (P.R.T.)

This system also uses off-line stations and small 2–6 person cabins, which run under computer control on a segregated guideway which is lightweight of small cross section and intended to be of low cost and built on a closely spaced grid throughout a city. The method of operation is as follows with most P.R.T. systems: (a.) passengers walk to their nearest station (b.) select their required station on a panel (c.) enter the vehicle when it arrives or the one waiting and (d.) proceed automatically to the station requested without interchange and with no intermediate stops. These systems operate precisely as they are named, for a passenger's personal use and base their small cabin size on average private car occupancy (often 1.3 passengers per car).

The P.R.T. systems under development differ from one another in detailed design and operation. Estimated capacities vary from 3–15,000 persons an hour in each direction and several systems are under trial on demonstration tracks. The U.S. system by TTI-Otis uses air cushion vehicles which dock at stations by moving sideways, reducing the stations dimensions. The German Cabinen-Taxi system (CAT) uses a single beam carrying vehicles running on top and slung below for two-way operation. The Japanese CVS system allows for

tracks to intersect at right angles in the same plane
so eliminating the need for two level flyovers at
junctions. The French Aramis system by Matra
runs vehicles in trains, like the Val system, and
uses magnetic couplings and an 0.5 second
headway to allow individual vehicles to leave the
train bound for different destinations.

The two new systems described G.R.T. and P.R.T.
have totally different characteristics. The first
(G.R.T.) assumes large vehicles operating on a
limited network of guideways with stations often
beyond walking distance from origin to passengers
destination. P.R.T. uses small cabins which run
on an intensive network of guideways so that no
point within the city is more than five minutes walk
from a station. This is undoubtedly the ultimate
system, which if capital costs could be kept low
enough, and could be met, might prove so
attractive to all members of a community as to
eliminate the need for intra-city private car use. It
does however assume that elevated guideways
would be acceptable over a great many city streets.
Estimates of capital cost vary enormously between
systems, and all cost estimates for G.R.T. and
P.R.T. systems are very optimistic with some less
than the cost of conventional rapid transit, some
only half the cost. It now seems important that
experience should be obtained with actual
installations in parts of a city where the transport
benefits to the community can be properly
established, and the visual impact assessed.

Study of CVS system running at low
level above a pedestrian street in the
Ginza district of Tokyo.

Japan's CVS system uses 2-4 seater
cars centrally guided, permitting
intersections at right angles to be made
in the same plane. A test track with 100
vehicles will be under trial in spring
1974.
*Japan Society for the Promotion of Machine
Industry.*

View of Cabinen-Taxi station on left superimposed on
an existing street in Hagen, Germany. Single guideway
permits cabins to run above and below.

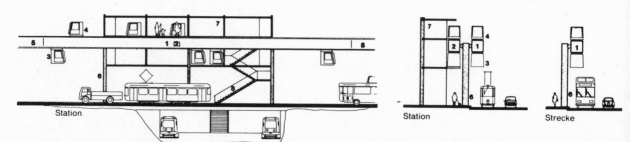

Section showing interchange between Cabinen-Taxi,
tram and underground railway.

Test track and station design for Hagen showing cabins being ordered on demand. Three person cabins are used, travelling at 36 km/h (22 mph).

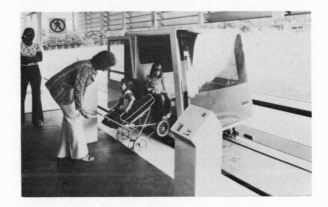

Closely spaced networks of Cabinen-Taxi, system shows that a maximum 350 metre walk to a station would be possible.
Demag-MBB.

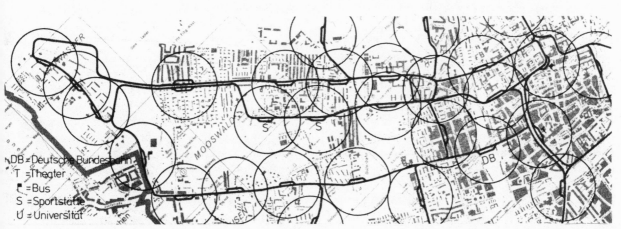

DB = Deutsche Bundesbahn
T = Theater
L = Bus
S = Sportstätte
U = Universität

Buses are a flexible and economic form of transport which given road space to move are likely to remain one of the most useful of any transport system. They can be used in a number of different ways:
1. as a primary system of transport for long and medium distance travel
2. as a secondary system of feeding into or from another system such as rapid-transit
3. as a local distribution system.

Operation: The most essential factor of good bus operation is that they should be given adequate road space free from congestion in order that they can run at good speeds and be reliable and many alternative ways are being found to make this possible. Given ideal motorway conditions buses can move over 20,000 passengers an hour, or more comparable to light rapid-transit, at an average speed, with frequent stops of up to 28 mph. For example, New York's busiest bus-only lane carries 25,800 people an hour on 500 buses and this kind of service is being tried in several cities in North America where excellent freeways exist. One example is the Blue Streak service in Seattle, Washington where a 'park and ride' service carries 500 commuters from a peripheral car park eight miles into the central area, with the buses entering the freeway on an exclusive ramp. Another experiment on the Shirley Highway, near Washington, D.C. uses five miles of exclusive bus-only highway on which buses can travel at 50 mph, cutting ten minutes off previous journey time in each direction.

In new towns it is possible to provide bus-only roads and to plan pedestrian routes around bus stops at the planning stage. Runcorn, England is an example (pages 49–52) where a twelve mile long busway will permit buses to operate at twice their normal average speeds (21 mph) and bus stops are a maximum five minute walk from homes. A similar concept is being applied to a new residential area housing eventually 8,000 people at Vallas, Sweden, where a 2,500 metre long busway runs through the pedestrian zone at the heart of rather than on the peripheral roads, saving a substantial annual mileage and by running on a ten minute frequency is likely to cause little disturbance to pedestrians. In many existing housing areas, often planned without consideration of bus operation, link roads for bus-only use may be built with automatic gates controlled by the buses, which allow them to pass through and collect or distribute passengers over a wider area. Buses are now using this on-board electronic equipment to activate traffic lights in their favour (page 91) as they approach a junction and 500 buses in London are being equipped with such devices which have been found in one experiment to reduce delays by twenty seconds at a single junction. On existing roads in cities which are heavily congested by traffic, buses can rarely attain average speeds of more than 10–12 mph although many schemes are providing them with priority over other vehicles. For example in a system in Southampton, England, along a three mile length of existing radial road, the signals on all roads entering this road have been modified and put under computer control. Detection pads in the main road record the level of traffic which is kept down to its maximum peak flow and the number of vehicles turning onto the road are restricted except for buses which mix with the other traffic. Bus-only lanes are also being

Road train specially designed for use at Whipsnade Zoo, near London.

Below:

Section through proposed bus station for City of Southampton, (see also page 35) showing

(1) roof garden   (2) concourse with shops
(3) waiting/seating area   (4) illuminated destination board   (5) warm air curtain   (6) loading platform.
Architect: Brian Richards — Consultant Engineers: Ove Arup & Partners.

University of Massachusetts at Amherst has enforced parking controls through pricing, charging $50 fee for 12 months in the centre, while peripheral car parks are free.

Computerised vehicle tracking system monitors automatically on a television screen the position of each bus and if it is running on time. Controller is in radio contact with drivers. *Marconi Company.*

provided in many cities, either running with the traffic flow or in counterflow lanes on one-way streets as in Piccadilly, London (page 85), which eliminates other vehicles illegally using the bus lane. It is estimated that bus-only lanes only require 60–70 buses an hour using them to be shown to be economic. Bus-only roads are now provided within pedestrian improvement schemes, as for example at Nicollet Mall, Minneapolis (page 8), where pavements were widened and landscaped, narrowing the road sufficiently to permit two-way operation.

Control: Bus fleets are now being equipped with two-way radios enabling drivers to be in constant touch with the central controller and to inform him of the buses' positions or where severe traffic congestion is causing the bus to run late so that reserve buses can be called up. In controlling large fleets, while voice communication is still important it is more difficult and automatic vehicle location systems are used of different kinds, which transmit the bus's location back to the control room automatically by radio and by using a computer identify its position on a television screen. Hamburg has since 1966 been using a system which compares each bus's location on a visual display unit with the ideal schedule alongside making it easy for a controller to see where a bus is running late and take appropriate action. Such control systems have many benefits, reducing the number of inspectors required, enabling information on bus operation to be continually recorded, and increase the morale of drivers. The morale of waiting passengers is equally important and in Tokyo a computerised vehicle location system is in use on seventy-four buses along five routes connected to electric signs at the bus stops which automatically light up when a particular bus has left the previous stop.

Fares: Alternative systems of fare collection are now being tried, designed to reduce delays at boarding points, (a one second reduction in stop time in Central London it is estimated could save £5 million annually using 1966 data) and facilitate one-man operation which still represents 65–75% of the cost of operating a bus. Interchangeable weekly or monthly tickets are being used on rail or bus by some authorities capable of being pre-bought at machines at bus stops or in local shops and cancelled on entering. Others use two-stream boarding, enabling passengers with correct change to use machines, or buy their tickets from drivers. Experiments too are being made with free fares usually for short distance travel and Nottingham, England, runs ten air-conditioned free shoppers' buses at five minute intervals around its central area carrying 90,000 passengers a week. An important experiment is also being tried using free shuttle buses at the University of Massachusetts at Amherst in an effort to improve the environment of the campus by a reduction in the numbers of cars parked.

Design: Modern buses are being made to an increasingly high standard of design, both fast and comfortable to ride on. For example the American Transbus has only a six inch entry step with wide well-illuminated doorways to reduce boarding times and make it easier for the handicapped and

88

aged to use. Special efforts too are being made to reduce the noise level inside and out by using quieter, well-insulated engines and double glazing, and air conditioning is now used widely in European buses. New methods of propulsion are being studied to reduce pollution using electric power, and steam or liquid gas as alternative fuels. A wide variety of bus sizes are now available and both France and North America are considering using double decker buses on busy routes. The problem of maximising on vehicles and manpower at off-peak periods still requires serious consideration and if special trailers or compartments were provided at least certain goods could be delivered by small buses. Several types of minibus have been developed for use in residential areas (see dial-a-ride) or within pedestrian areas where they are popular with shoppers but costly to run and unable to handle peak loads.

Trailer trains or road trams are widely used at exhibitions, parks or within pedestrian areas and are capable of carrying large numbers of people. At Disney World, Florida, road trams carry 150 people at a time in three open trailers seating five abreast as a shuttle service between car parks and ticket barriers. The zoo trains, specially built for Whipsnade Zoo near London, have the capability of turning through a tight radius and may eventually run along pedestrian routes.

Infrastructure: Buildings associated with bus operation require to provide as high a level of comfort as the bus itself, particularly where the service is infrequent. American proposals suggest shelters might be fully enclosed, ideally heated and entered by means of the ticket, also used on the

Electric signs at bus stops in Tokyo controlled by central
computer which keep track of all buses along their route
and show waiting passengers time next bus will arrive.
Yoshio Tsukio

bus. Seats and good lighting combined with all
relevant information about services are equally
important, and illuminated signs installed such as
those now operating in Tokyo.

Dual-mode operation
The guideway used by personal rapid-transit
systems represents 60–70% of the total capital
cost of the system and led in the early 1960's to
pioneering work by William Alden in the United

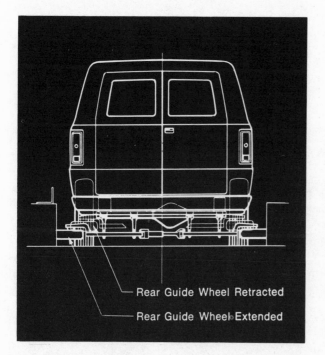

Rear Guide Wheel Retracted

Rear Guide Wheel Extended

States on the development of a small battery-powered car, the Starrcar, which could be driven on roads in the normal way or enter a guideway and run at high speeds under automatic guidance and control together with other vehicles confined permanently to the guideway. Guideways could thus be maximised and networks more widely spaced if vehicles could be driven onto them at stations so avoiding the need for passengers to interchange. A minibus, for example, operating on a dial-a-ride basis would collect passengers at their home, drive to the nearest station, enter a guideway and proceed driverless under computer control dropping passengers at their selected stations while the driver took another vehicle and made a further round. Another use of the dual-

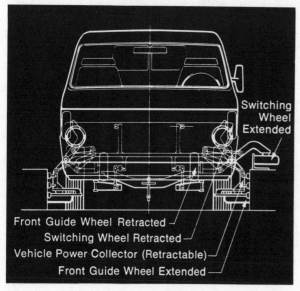

Switching
Wheel
Extended

Front Guide Wheel Retracted
Switching Wheel Retracted
Vehicle Power Collector (Retractable)
Front Guide Wheel Extended

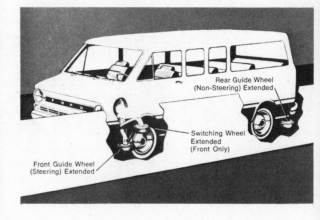

Rear Guide Wheel
(Non-Steering) Extended

Switching Wheel
Extended
(Front Only)

Front Guide Wheel
(Steering) Extended

Ford ACT system, shown as a potential dual-mode system, using a minibus, capable of being modified to run under automatic guidance and control on a track.

a INTERROGATOR
b LOCAL DECODER
c POWER SUPPLY

TO INTERSECTION CONTROLLER

CONTROL BOX

BATTERY

TRANSPONDER

Buses can be fitted with equipment enabling drivers to operate traffic-lights in their favour.
Philips Telecommunicatie Industrie B.V.

mode system would be for light deliveries, refuse and mail collection and delivery where the longer part of the total journey to or from warehouse, sorting office or depot could be by driverless vehicle on the guideway, collected by drivers at stations and then used on the local roads.

Contracts were let by the U.S. Government in 1973 to Rohr, General Motors and TTI-Otis for dual-mode development and if the results are successful a system is to be introduced into revenue service by 1980. In cities where extensive freeways already exist it would be possible for one traffic lane in each direction to be converted into an automated guideway as well as separate guideways constructed capable of being entered at or exited from take-off points at convenient intervals. The principle advantage of this solution is that as control systems are developed, automated guideways can carry many more vehicles safely by permitting closer spacing and by using electric power eliminate atmospheric pollution.

Apart from the Starrcar, the Airtrans system operational at Dallas/Fort Worth airport has vehicles designed to carry containers for mail, goods or refuse capable of being towed off the guideways in the event of a breakdown or within the maintenance area for ease in servicing. A self-powered vehicle has also been designed for dual-mode operation. Ford's ACT system also allows for a twelve seat bus to be equipped with guidance and power collection and run on a guideway. Dual-mode operation appears to be the ultimate development of the G.R.T. system and could be introduced when it appeared economic to pay for the extra cost of altering freeways and equipping road vehicles with two motors, power steering and control mechanism all capable of being checked electronically before entering a guideway.

All the innovations described are designed to ensure that existing or new bus transport running along fixed routes can run on time and prove attractive to passengers. In certain areas, not planned around fixed-route bus operation walking distances to or from bus stops may be long, and so require a more flexible system of bus operation called dial-a-ride. This consists of a number of minibuses equipped with radio, and controlled from a central control room staffed with telephone operators, and others responsible for scheduling calls, and dispatching the vehicles. The system works in the following way: a prospective passenger phones into the dial-a-ride control centre his request, for example to visit the shopping centre, or go to the rapid transit station. The operator checks with the scheduler that a bus is close by and going in the required direction and informs the caller when he will be picked up. All this is recorded on a wall map and the bus driver informed on the radio telephone whom he is to pick up next. This done, the driver informs the control centre he is proceeding to the caller's house and when he has picked up his passenger proceeds towards his destination. There are many permutations to the system which can be used at different times of day, depending on demand. At peak hours for example, half the buses in the fleet may operate as feeder systems to or from a bus or rail-rapid transit stop, or on a fixed route with pre-arranged stops, like an ordinary bus and only being diverted from this route when requested to by the controller to pick up a passenger, called a few-to-many system of operation. Alternatively, during the day a wide variety of trips may be required by passengers to visit shops or libraries, or other houses called a many-to-many operation.

Regular users of the system, for example commuters, are encouraged to pre-book their requirements which can improve the operation and help to reduce their waiting time. An important aspect of the system is that although it can be used in any existing area, it is in areas which have been well planned and where activities are clustered that more economic systems of dial-a-ride can run. The system, normally tailored to a community may vary in size and use straightforward radio-control to the drivers. For example the system at Regina, Saskatchewan, started in 1971 with six buses operating in an area of $2\frac{1}{2}$ square miles controlled by two operators, while at Haddonfield, New Jersey, eighteen vehicles are operating in an area of eleven square miles controlled by four operators, in both the drivers are in speech-contact with the operators. A more complex system is now in use at Rochester, New York, where the driver no longer requires to be controlled by radio telephone and instead reads off his order on a print-out situated in his cabin. Scheduling and dispatching eventually will come under computer control and should mean a reduction in control staff and a much more efficient operation. Ultimately it is suggested that a completely press-button operation could be arranged with the passengers simply dialling their required destination, and this could overcome the problem of households having no telephones. Although up to 90% of telephone ownership exists in the U.S., this is lower in Europe, often only 50% in U.K. so that special street telephone booths require to be set up at each street corner with direct lines to the control centre.

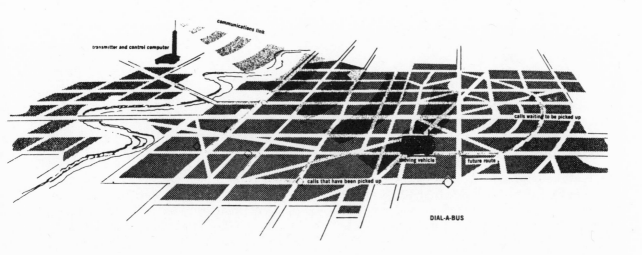

communications link

transmitter and control computer

calls waiting to be picked up

moving vehicle future route

calls that have been picked up

DIAL-A-BUS

Dial-a-ride systems use a radio-controlled minibus and circulate in residential areas collecting or dropping off passengers who have phoned for service.
U.S. Dept. of Housing & Urban Development.

Example of dial-a-ride literature used at experiment in Haddonfield, New Jersey, to inform residents of system.

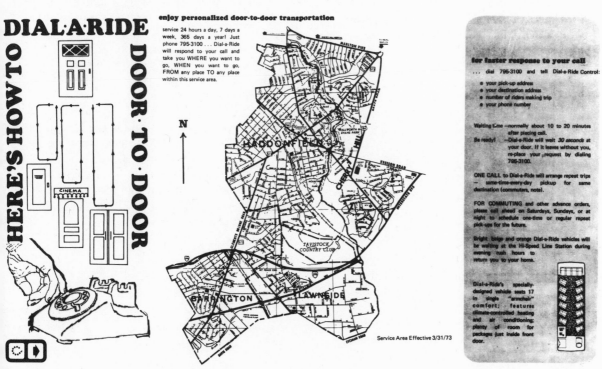

DIAL·A·RIDE

DOOR·TO·DOOR

HERE'S HOW TO

enjoy personalized door-to-door transportation

service 24 hours a day, 7 days a week, 365 days a year! Just phone 795-3100 . . . Dial-a-Ride will respond to your call and take you WHERE you want to go, WHEN you want to go, FROM any place TO any place within this service area.

N

HADDONFIELD

BARRINGTON   LAWNSIDE

Service Area Effective 3/31/73

for faster response to your call

. . . dial 795-3100 and tell Dial-a-Ride Control:

● your pick-up address
● your destination address
● number of riders making trip
● your phone number

Waiting time —normally about 10 to 20 minutes after placing call.
Be ready! —Dial-a-Ride will wait *30 seconds* at your door. If it leaves without you, re-place your request by dialing 795-3100.

ONE CALL to Dial-a-Ride will arrange repeat trips — same-time-every-day pickup for same destination (commuters, note).

FOR COMMUTING and other advance orders, please call ahead on Saturdays, Sundays, or at night to schedule one-time or regular repeat pick-ups for the future.

Bright beige and orange Dial-a-Ride vehicles will be waiting at the Hi-Speed Line Station during evening rush hours to return you to your home.

Dial-a-Ride's specially-designed vehicle seats 17 in single "armchair" comfort; features climate-controlled heating and air conditioning; plenty of room for packages just inside front door.

Taxis and Jitneys

Taxis are an important system of personal transport which can be hailed from the pavement edge or requested for by telephone and carry the passengers, with his luggage, parcels, dogs, pram and children from door to door with no intermediate stops. Although the cost of this service is higher than one by public transport or private car it has none of the latter's parking problems and may mean that many of the more affluent city dwellers may prefer not to own their own car, using taxis when required, or hiring a car for weekend use.

There are however several improvements which could be made to conventional taxi operation:

i).   Taxis could be better designed to suit their real requirements with mini-taxis seating 2-3 for average use taking up less road space and maxi-taxis seating 7-8 for shared taxi operation. Non-polluting engines should be obligatory.

ii).   Radio telephones should connect each taxi with one central control room.

iii).   Taxi stands should be provided at every rapid transit or bus station, as well as being strategically placed at frequent intervals throughout the town or city, each one equipped with a telephone connected by direct-line to the central control room. This should permit empty cruising taxis to be eliminated.

iv). Relaxation and simplification of licensing laws which now limit the number of taxis could allow more to operate, avoid the often expensive license fee (in New York "medallion" drivers pay $20,000 to operate) and so satisfy the increasing demand for their use.

Jitney taxis, often called service taxis, carry several passengers who share the same vehicle which normally runs on a fixed route although running on shorter headways than a bus, displays a card stating the route and picks up or drops passengers at any point they require, occasionally deviating from the route if especially requested. Transport authorities in Munich, Germany, and Besançon, France are now subsidising private firms to run jitney taxis at night in lower density residential areas as an alternative to running buses. In Teheran, Mexico City and many others, jitney taxis consisting of large cars represent an essential part of the cities transport system with fares between conventional taxis and buses. In other cities such as Atlantic City and San Francisco small vans are used seating 10-14 people. Jitney operation has in the past been seriously curtailed by legal action enacted by the public transport operators and in the U.S. in 1915 it was estimated that 62,000 illegal jitneys were operating. There now seems a strong case for encouraging experiments with jitneys operating particularly along routes which bus operators find uneconomic, and from points such as rail or air terminals in competition with taxis.

Subscription services and car pools

There is a single demand for transport services to be tailored to the requirements of the community and a variety of alternatives have been operating for many years.

(i).   The subscription bus service where a number of people in the community, which is badly served by public transport, may club together and pay for a private bus operator to run a service to a town, city or interchange point with express rail or bus. Reston in the United States, a new residential community of 23,000 people is an example where regular commuter ridership has built up to 17,000 passenger trips per day into Washington in 5 years. Subscription services similarly extend to dial-a-ride for example where a daily pick-up is required at the same time each day, to carry a child to school or a commuter to a rail station and this represents a very economic use of the system.

(ii).   The community bus is an alternative approach where a small community clubs together and purchases a minibus to be used for shopping trips or visits for old people, and driven by one of the local residents. The Eastern Counties Bus Company in Norfolk, England, recently purchased such a vehicle for exclusive use by one village from which the bus service had been withdrawn.

(iii).   Van pools are similar in concept except that they are normally organised by an industrial plant or large office who purchase a fleet of vans and match the workers living in the same neighbourhoods to share the same van. The 3M Company in St. Paul, Minnesota is an example of this operation where 12 passenger vans were supplied to employees, one of whom is responsible for driving the van and collecting fares, having the use of the van himself and paying no fare. The vans are allowed free close-in parking at the factory, an important incentive where large ground-level parking exists and 340 parking spaces have been saved since the introduction of the van pool.

iv).   Car pools have long existed in their simplest form for carrying children to and from school and since the fuel crisis in 1973 a number of experiments, chiefly in the United States, have met with varying degrees of success. One of the most important factors in car pooling is the efficiency of the information service which matches the riders travel needs. Apart from obvious savings in car running costs or the fact that non-car owning riders can be served, there are strong incentives in terms of actual travel time to be gained from car-pooling where they are permitted to use bus lanes, or at toll bridges where priority is given. On the San Francisco/Oakland Bay Bridge two priority lanes were allocated to cars carrying 3 or more people (see page 10) and the 50 cent toll changed to one dollar per month. Doubling of the shared cars was also to some extent initiated by giving drivers postcard application forms for car-pool matching.

All the services and systems described above are designed to give mobility to people who do not necessarily own their own private cars or are too old or young to use one and can either complement the existing public transport service or be used as an alternative where it does not exist.

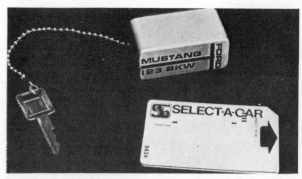

B

Select-a-car hire system in U.S. showing (a) remote
station (b) Select-a-Car credit card and 'key-unit'. (c)
Steering column mounted for 'key unit' including
odometer. (d) Central data station which produces
account. *Minicars Inc.*

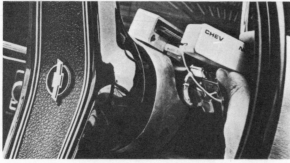

C

D

Car Hire

Car hire is already an important industry
providing licence holders with convenient
transport at airports, or railway and bus stations
at low cost. Several proposals and experiments
have been made to develop ways of so simplifying
car hire, that it could be used in a city for those
cross-city trips made on business or shopping,
where time is important, and samples or parcels
may have to be carried. The U.S. Dept. of
Transportation sponsored development by
Minicars Inc. where a credit card is issued to a
subscriber who inserts it into a 'remote station'
when he wishes to hire a car, releasing a 'key unit'
with which to unlock the car and by inserting the

96

'odometer' starts it. The car is driven, for as long
as required, and left at a convenient 'station',
the 'key unit' returned and the credit card
processed, with the length of time the car is used
recorded on the odometer, then transmitted to a
data bank enabling the subscriber to be billed
monthly. In Montpellier, France a simple version
of this was tried using thirty-seven conventional
cars by a society called PROCOTIP. Subscribers
paid the equivalent of $42 for a key giving them
access to any available car, and purchased plastic
counters which were inserted into the TIP
meter allowing them eleven miles of driving. The
system failed for several reasons, partly through

A

B

Witkar short-term car hire system proposed for
Amsterdam consists of (a) parking at special areas for up
to 10 vehicles which can be charged from above
(b) Witkar, 2 seater + baggage battery operated vehicle
(c) selection pole where required station is requested and
key issued if parking space available.
C. V. Witkar – Amsterdam.

lack of finance, and because cars were left at
random points rather than in the areas specially
marked out, which were often filled with illegally
parked cars. In Amsterdam, the Witkar system is

C

being introduced, by Lund Schimmelpenninck
who tried to introduce the principle of free white
bicycles into a car-free centre. This uses an
electric two-seater car (plus room for a child and
packages) which is parked in-line with others at
special ranks where overhead battery charging
can take place. Subscribers pay an initial charge
the equivalent of £7 (about $16) giving them a
credit card, and when this is inserted into the
'selection pole' and the required rank dialled, the
driver is given a key, provided space is available,
and the first car in the rank is then driven off.
A charge of ten cents a minute is made and average
travel distance estimated at between one and
two-and-a-half miles with initially five ranks
being installed for thirty-five cars, extended as
and when required. Such a system introduced on
a city-wide scale, could by maximising vehicles,
road and parking space, provide a useful vehicle
for many kinds of trip and help make a total ban
on private cars more acceptable, at certain times
of day in central areas.

Cycling is becoming increasingly popular both for commuting and pleasure in Europe and is on the increase in North America where the number of cycles sold annually is expected to equal if not pass car sales in 1974, a 100% rise in the last ten years. Partly this is due to the increases in leisure, concern for the environment and to improved cycle design, the introduction of mini-bikes which are easily stored and development of five and ten speed lightweight cycles capable of coping with hills.

In European cities, cycling already accounts for a high proportion of total trips. In Copenhagen for example in 1971 one million out of a total 6 million daily trips were made on cycles and in Rotterdam 43% of all trips are made on cycles. In the North American cities, while cycling in the journey to work is still undertaken by relatively few, one spectacular example exists at Davis, California, where an estimated 10,000 people ride to and from the campus daily, compared to Washington D.C. where an estimated 1,200 fair weather cyclists commute eight months in the year, and the Smithsonian plan proposes a well-reasoned series of cycleways leading from three residential areas. It is now recognised that cyclist require specially designed road space for reasons of safety and comfort and three types of cycleway have been classified in a study undertaken for the California Department of Public Works.

Class 1. A completely separated right of way used only by cyclists with grade-separated intersections with other roads. These are often now provided in parks, or planned into new development. For

example in Peterborough, England, an expanding new city, at present 22% of all work journeys are made by cycle and a new seventy-two mile cycleway is being planned specifically to try and keep cycling a popular mode of travel. Stevenage, England, has twenty-three miles of cycleway with ninety underpasses and here an estimated 9% cycle regularly to work and there are 4,000 regular cyclists in the town. The cycleways here are built twelve feet wide, and are shared with pedestrians except at underpasses, which are made by lowering the track four feet and raising the road six feet to avoid steep ramps.

Class 2. These are cycleways provided in built-up areas physically separated by a pavement or verge from the main road and at junctions provided either with light controls to give cyclists safe crossing or various designs of crossings at the same level as the road. There are many examples in Europe of Class 2 cycleways and reason to believe they provide a safe system. For example in Copenhagen such a cycle track 5 km. long produced a 60% lower rate of accident than one without a track, where cycles mixed with the traffic. Ideally one-way tracks are provided on each side of the road at least two cycle lanes wide, around 5ft. 3 inches wide (1.6 metres) capable of carrying 2–4,000 cycles an hour in each direction.

Class 3. This cycleway shares the road space alongside and has road markings with sign posts to indicate its position. This is the least satisfactory form of track and assumes that kerbside parking can be eliminated and controlled. Another alternative with wider environmental benefits is to reduce the speed and number of vehicles on

Cycling in Amsterdam.
Klein.

existing roads, by using 'humps' designed to let cycles through and by traffic management (see Gothenburg page 13) where cyclists are allowed certain priorities permitting them to wheel cycles between 'zones' where through roads have been blocked off. One Gothenburg hotel, incidentally encourages its clientele to cycle by providing them with the use of white mini-bikes at no charge.

Measures designed to make the cycling environment safer and more pleasant encourage people to cycle more. New York city for example by banning cars in Central Park on Sundays has recorded 10,000 people being on cycles in one single day. Provisions for adequate parking of cycles is also important, and many enlightened transit authorities now provide cycle racks at stations or bus stops and recognise that short of walking this is an extremely 'economic' feeder system, capable of parking 14–16 cycles in a space occupied by one car. Housing too requires lock-up space for cycles for the whole family directly adjoining the road or path where the cycle will be used.

Authorities are responding rapidly to often well-considered proposals made by cycle clubs and communities for a better cycling environment, and recognise that by so doing, this could prove to be an inexpensive solution to the traffic problem and become for many people a useful and enjoyable way of moving in cities.

A folding cycle that can be stored in its own carrying case.
Carnielli and C. Milan.

Acknowledgments

The research on early systems of movement was done under a Nuffield Foundation Grant and is published by permission of Professor Sir Colin Buchanan.

The Soho Study by Dean and myself was done as part of the London Roads Study 1959 by Alison and Peter Smithson.

The London Bridge Study was done by myself with Ove Arup and Partners as Consulting Engineers and is published by permission of Dunlop Transportation Systems Division.

The Study for La Defense was done by Ove Arup and Partners with myself as architect and Jean Prouve as consultant and is published by permission of the French Authority EPAD.

Particular help was given by members of the following organizations.

British Hydromechanics Research Association.

Greater London Council.

Transport and Road Research Laboratory.

Thanks are also due to Roger Slevin, Yoshio Tsukio, Curt Elmberg, and many others who gave advice and the manufacturers who supplied material.

Special thanks to Bill Harrison who drew many of the diagrams, Joan Brown who typed the script and at Whitecross Studios to Jonathan Bosley and my wife, Sandra Lousada who took many of the photographs.

COMPARATIVE PLANS OF TRANSPORT SYSTEMS	COMPARATIVE SECTIONS FOR TWO WAY OPERATION	TURNING RADII	ECONOMIC DISTANCE BETWEEN STOPS OR STATIONS	PASSENGER OR VEHICLE CAPACITY PER HOUR ONE WAY	AVERAGE SPEED
PEDESTRIANS				10-15,000	4.8 km/h 3 mph
BICYCLES				2-5,000	16 km/h 10 mph
PRIVATE CAR ON SURFACE STREET IN CITY				700-900 vph	13-24 km/h 8-15 mph
MINIBUS		6m 20'	400-800m .24-.48 mile	120 vph 3,600	10-15 km/h 6-30 mph
OPEN BUS TRAILER		8m 26'	as required	100 vph 7,500	13 km/h 8 mph
EXPRESS BUS ON GRADE SEPARATED ROAD		20m 66'	1,610m 1mile	1,450 vph 60,000	88.5 km/h 55 mph
DOUBLE DECK BUS ON SURFACE STREET IN CITY		21.3m 70'	330m .2 mile	120 vph 7,200	13-24 km/h 8-15 mph
VEC SYSTEM		25m 82'	300-500m .18-.3 mile	1,000-1,500	12-20 km/h 7-13 mph
POMA 2000		10m 33'	400m .24 mile	4,500-8,000	35 km/h 22 mph
MINIRAIL		24.5m 80'	800m .5 mile	4-10,000	50-64.5 km/h 30-40 mph

Scales:
COMPARATIVE PLANS — metres 0 5 10 20 40; feet 0 10 50 100
COMPARATIVE SECTIONS — metres 0 1 5 10; feet 0 5 10 20 30

Comparative plans and section of urban transport
systems drawn to two different scales.

Comparative plans of transport systems	Comparative sections for two way operation	Turning radii	Economic distance between stops or stations	Passenger or vehicle capacity per hour one way	Average speed
CARVEYOR (8 passenger)		3.7m 12'	400m .24 mile	8,000	19 km/h 12 mph
TELEPHERIQUE GONDOLA CAR (4 seat car)		straight	1.610m min 1mile "	500-1000	9.6-16.1 km/h 6-10 mph
PEDESTRIAN CONVEYOR OR MOVING BELT		straight	100m .06 mile	7,500	2.5-3 km/h 1.5-1.9 mph
SPEEDAWAY		straight	400m .24 mile	~10,000	12-16.1 km/h 7.5-10 mph
PRT TTI-OTIS		22.4m 80'	400-800m .24-.48 mile	15,000	30-50 km/h 18-30 mph
PRT CABINENTAXI		30m 99'	300-800m .18-.48 mile	9-15,000	36 km/h 22.5 mph
AIRTRANS		25m 82'	400-800m .24-.48 mile	9000	30-55 km/h 18-34 mph
MONORAIL (Alweg-Hitachi)		46m 150'	800m min 5mile "	16-20,000	80 km/h 50 mph
TRANSIT EXPRESSWAY (Westinghouse)		46m 150'	800-3,200m .5-2 mile	8-20,000	36-63 km/h 23-39 mph
UNDERGROUND RAILWAY (London system)		101m 330'	800-3,200m .5-2 mile	40,000	32-50 km/h 20-30 mph
ARTICULATED THREE CAR TRAM		15-30m 50-100'	400-800m .25-.5 mile	20,000	32-50 km/h 20-30 mph

metres 0 5 10 20 40
feet 0 10 50 100

metres 0 1 5 10
feet 0 5 10 20 30

The Pedestrian

Personal Mobility and Transport Policy.
M. Hillman, PEP, 12 Upper Belgrave Street,
London. 1973.
Planning for disabled people in the urban
environment. Central Council for the Disabled,
London 1969.
Pedestrianised Streets, Greater London Council.
County Hall, London, SE1. 1973.
Streets for people   OECD.
Paris. 1974.
More Streets for People: Italian Art and
Landscape Foundation Inc. 660 Madison Avenue,
New York. 1973.
Pedestrian. Planning and Design. J. J. Fruin.
MAUDEP. P.O. Box 722. Church Street Station,
New York. N.Y. 10008. 1971.
Streets for People. B Rudofsky. Doubleday, New
York. 1969.
Environmental Quality of City Streets.
D. Appleyard & M. Lintell. Institute of Urban
and Regional Development. University of
California. Berkeley. 1970.
The Image of the City. K. Lynch. M.I.T. Press.
1960.

Pedestrian transport

Passenger conveyors. J. Tough. C. O'Flaherty.
Ian Allen. London. 1971.
Transportation of Man. S. Asmervik. Institute of
City and Regional Planning Technical University
of Norway. Trondheim 1970.
Transportation systems for Major Activity
Centres. OECD. Paris. 1970.
Movement in Cities. B. Richards. Architects Year
Book 12. Urban Structure. Elek. London. **1968**.

Urban Design Manhattan. Regional Plan
Association. Studio Vista. London. 1969.
Mini-systems in the City. B. Richards.
Architectural Forum. January, 1968.

Transport: General

Towns against Traffic: S. Plowden. Deutsch.
London. 1972.
Changing Directions, Report of Independent
Commission on Transport. Coronet Books.
London 1974.
Future Urban Transportation Systems. Vols. 1–2
Stanford Research Institute, Menlo Park,
California. 1968.
Bibliography: Unconventional Passenger
Transportation Systems U.I.T.P. Avenue de
l'Uruguay 19. B-1050 Brussels. Belgium. 1973.
The Transport Gaps. Bouladon. Science
Journal (April) London. 1967.
Tomorrows Transportation. US Dept. of Housing
and Urban Development. Washington D.C. 1968.

Transport: Technical

Personal Rapid Transit. J. E. Anderson et al.
Depts of Audio Visual Extension, University of
Minnesota. April 1972.
The Horizontal Elevator. B. Richards.
Architectural Design. June. London. 1971.
Development in Personal Rapid Transit.
B. Richards. Architectural Design. March.
London. 1974.
Urban Public Transport: Service Innovations in
Operation Planning and Technology. R.A. Burco.
OECD. Paris. 1972.
Personal and Group Rapid Transit Systems and
Technologies. Selected bibliography. C. Henderson.
Stanford Research Institute, Menlo Park.
California. 94025.

DATE DUE

DISPLAY			
NOV 15 '7?			
OCT 31 '7?			
FEB 6 '79			
FEB 6 '79			
FEB 27 '79			
FEB 28 '79			
ILL due 6-9-90			
GAYLORD			PRINTED IN U.S.A.